Presented to:

_____

From:

_____

with Dr. David Jeremiah

Unless otherwise indicated, Scripture verses quoted are from the
NEW KING JAMES VERSION.

Printed in the United States of America.

*Answers to
Questions About*

SPIRITUAL
WARFARE

DAVID JEREMIAH

Table of Contents

God's Armory   69

The Girdle of Truth   72

Introduction

*M*icroeconomics is about your checkbook; *macro*economics is about global financial markets. There is a big picture and a small picture to everything—even the spiritual life.

Understandably, most people focus on the *micro* issues in life—what's happening to me today. But without a solid biblical backdrop (the *macro* view), today's challenges can be misunderstood and discouraging. The biblical backdrop for viewing all of life's events is called spiritual warfare—the ages-old conflict between the kingdom of darkness and the kingdom of light. Paul says in Colossians 1:13 that God "has delivered us from the power of darkness and conveyed us into the kingdom of the Son of His love."

The ruler of the powers of darkness, Satan, is none too happy about what God has accomplished in Christ. His main goal is to destroy the faith of Christians by getting them to doubt God's goodness, love, forgiveness, protection, provision, and promises. When Satan creates difficult circumstances in our life, it is not just to inflict pain; it is for the purpose of destroying our trust in God.

We know from Scripture that Satan will not win the spiritual war, but every time he gets a Christian to give up on God, he wins a spiritual battle. The Bible begins (Genesis 3:1-5) and ends (Revelation 20:8) with Satan attempting to deceive humanity *in order to make God look bad*.

Answers to Questions About Spiritual Warfare reveals Satan's strategies against God and man—the big picture. But it also describes the Christian's path to spiritual victory: how to defeat Satan's attacks and remain faithful to God in life's most challenging moments.

While Satan has been given temporary freedom to oppose God in this world (1 John 5:19), Christ came to ultimately destroy his efforts (1 John 3:8). In the interim, God gives us promises and power by which we can win every spiritual battle (1 Corinthians 10:13).

Terms of Engagement

Fight the
good fight
of faith.

1 Timothy 6:12

Why study spiritual warfare?

Biblically and practically speaking, we are in a spiritual war. The Christian's spiritual enemy is not in uniform, and he doesn't meet us on an identifiable battlefield. He uses ruthless and unconventional tactics, such as deceit, deflection, and disguise. A large number of pastors and teachers ignore or downplay spiritual warfare to the point that many professing Christians don't even know they're in a war. This puts Christians in serious danger. The Church of Jesus Christ needs to know its enemy and his strategies. And above all, Christians need to know how to gain victory over this enemy.

Two things are happening today that I never thought I would live to see. First, spiritual warfare is getting much more intense and Satan is becoming much more real. Second, as mentioned above, too many Christians are not taking spiritual warfare seriously or even believing such a war is going on. These two factors taken together mean we have a crisis on our hands. When the danger increases and awareness decreases, an alarm needs to be sounded to prevent disaster.

Are we really in a war?

Be assured, spiritual warfare is a reality in the life of every believer. When you open the pages of the New Testament, there is no shortage of passages that characterize the Christian as a warrior and the Christian life as a battle. We are called to a grim struggle with unseen forces, and the fight is real.

> "This charge I commit to you, son Timothy, according to the prophecies previously made concerning you, that by them you may wage the good warfare" (1 Timothy 1:18).

> "Fight the good fight of faith, lay hold on eternal life . . ." (1 Timothy 6:12).

> "I have fought the good fight, I have finished the race, I have kept the faith" (2 Timothy 4:7).

> "You therefore must endure hardship as a good soldier of Jesus Christ" (2 Timothy 2:3).

"No one engaged in warfare entangles himself with the affairs of *this* life, that he may please him who enlisted him as a soldier" (2 Timothy 2:4).

"Watch, stand fast in the faith, be brave, be strong" (1 Corinthians 16:13).

Commenting on these passages, J. C. Ryle writes, "Words such as these appear to me clear, plain, and unmistakable. They all teach one and the same great lesson, if we are willing to receive it. That lesson is, that true Christianity is a struggle, a fight, and a warfare."[1]

> Know it or not, like it or not,
> you and I are in a war!
> And we need to begin
> living as if we were
> in a battle for our lives.
> Because, in fact, we are.[2]
>
> *Stu Weber*

Don't Believe in a Devil

Men don't believe in a devil now,
*   As their fathers used to do;*
They've forced the door of the broadest creed
*   To let his majesty through;*
There isn't a print of his cloven foot,
*   Or a fiery dart from his bow,*
To be found in earth or air to-day,
*   For the world has voted so.*

But who is mixing the fatal draft
*   That palsies heart and brain,*
And loads the earth of each passing year
*   With ten hundred thousand slain?*
Who blights the bloom of the land to-day
*   With the fiery breath of hell,*
If the devil isn't and never was?
*   Won't somebody rise and tell?*

Alfred J. Hough[3]

Against whom are we fighting?

> My brethren, be strong in the Lord and in the power of His might. Put on the whole armor of God, that you may be able to stand against the wiles of the devil. For we do not wrestle against flesh and blood, but against principalities, against powers, against the rulers of the darkness of this age, against spiritual hosts of wickedness in the heavenly places.
>
> *Ephesians 6:10-12*

Every time Paul mentions another class of spiritual beings, he reaffirms that we wrestle *against* them. The word *against* appears six times in these three verses. Think of an oarsman rowing his boat *against* the current. He is trying to make progress in one direction while the current seeks to take him the opposite way. We are trying to make progress toward the kingdom of God, and Satan turns the current of the world in the opposite direction, resisting us with every stroke of the oar.

Satan's war against us is organized and complete with strategies. The word *principalities* (Ephesians 6:12) refers to his head officers, while the word *wiles* (verse 11) refers to clever plans, crafty deceptions, and cunning methods. Like a military general, Satan plans his attacks and directs his demonic forces.

Note carefully how Paul describes this one against whom we are fighting: "For we do not wrestle against flesh and blood." In other words, our enemies are not people. You may think they are, but they are not. John Phillips puts it this way:

> We must see beyond people. Satan may use people to persecute us, lie to us, cheat us, hurt us, or even kill us. But our real enemy lurks in the shadows of the unseen world, moving people as pawns on the chessboard of time. As long as we see people as enemies and wrestle against them, we will spend our strength in vain.[4]

Satan is the great destroyer. He wants to destroy

your life through adversity, getting in the way and blocking the moves that God wants to make in your life. He does that by discouragement, by dissipating your time and energy, and by a frontal assault on your weak areas to lead you to sin. Satan wants to disrupt your walk with God, ruin your testimony, and destroy your life.

Paul gives the following instruction in Ephesians chapter 6: "My brethren, be strong" (verse 10) Why? So we can get into this battle and fight against the enemy who is against us. This is not a fight for the apostles. This is not a fight for the pastors. This is not a fight for the deacons or the leaders. This is a fight for the brethren, for all of us together—the brothers and the sisters. The lines have been drawn. And our enemy, with whom we are involved in mortal combat, is none other than Satan himself. It is the Lord and the brethren against Satan and the demons.

How can I be certain I've been called to battle?

You may be wondering, *Maybe I haven't been called to this fight. You know, I'm really not the warrior type.* Well, you may not be acting like a warrior; but if you're a Christian, you're in the army. All believers have been drafted, and you're either going to help fight or you're going to stand in the background and be miserable.

J. C. Ryle has written these words:

> The true Christian is called to be a soldier and must behave as such from the day of his conversion to the day of his death. He is not meant to live a life of religious ease, indolence, and security. He must never imagine for a moment that he can sleep and doze along the way to heaven.[5]

It seems that much of the modern theology that we're being exposed to today is almost entirely about how we can make things better for ourselves: how we can get more money, how we can have more rest, how we can have better things, how we can do this and that. It's all about us. But when we study the Bible, we realize that it's not just about making us feel better. It's about making us be better soldiers of Jesus Christ. And that's the spirit of the godly soldier—not looking for the easiest way but asking for God's help to be prepared for what's ahead.

In order to know our enemy, we must understand how Satan goes about accomplishing his purposes. I paged through the Bible, writing down the verbs describing his activity: Satan beguiles, seduces, opposes, resists, deceives, sows terror, hinders, buffets, tempts, persecutes, blasphemes—and more. There are no edifying verbs associated with Satan. His determined goal is to diminish and deface the glory of God. And in pursuit of that goal he is utterly deceitful, divisive, and destructive.

All believers have been
drafted, and you're either
going to help fight or
you're going to stand
in the background and
be miserable.

How can I be a courageous warrior for God when I feel powerless?

Once we understand the fact that we're in a spiritual battle, one of the first thoughts that tends to come to mind is, *I am not capable of fighting in this war.* The reality is, this is a tough war. Letting fear or your own inadequacies keep you from the battle is not acceptable. Every Christian, regardless of age or maturity, is called by God's Word to be fearless. And we do not have to fear, because we are never going to be asked to fight this war on our own strength. God promises to strengthen us with His might.

In the book of Ephesians, the apostle Paul provides a word of encouragement: "My brethren, be strong in the Lord and in the power of His might" (Ephesians 6:10). And 2 Timothy 1:7 tells us that "God has not given us a spirit of fear, but of power." In these passages we are reminded that the strength and power for the battle is a gift from the Lord. Isn't that a great encouragement? God Almighty has promised us, as His soldiers, that He will protect us and keep us strong. We can therefore come boldly to the front lines, knowing that the Christian is not commanded to be courageous in his own strength but to be emboldened by the power of another—and that other is Jesus Christ.

More than a century ago, the Evangelical Anglican J. C. Ryle wrote:

> The saddest symptom about many so-called Christians is the utter absence of anything like conflict and fight in their Christianity. They eat, they drink, they dress, they work, they amuse themselves, they get money, they spend money, they go through a scanty round of formal religious services once or twice every week. But the great spiritual warfare—its watchings and strugglings, its agonies and anxieties, its battles and contests—of all this they appear to know nothing at all.[6]

The Christian is not
commanded to be
courageous in his own
strength but to be
emboldened by the
power of another—and
that other is Jesus Christ.

Behind
Enemy Lines

Be sober, be vigilant;
because your adversary
the devil walks about
like a roaring lion,
seeking whom he
may devour.

1 Peter 5:8

Why is it important to understand the enemy?

It's always a good thing before you fight a war to know something about the enemy you're fighting against. In the spiritual realm, it could never be more true. Many Christians do not take the enemy seriously because they don't know enough about him to take him seriously. In fact, Satan's cleverest strategy is to make us believe that he does not exist. Some Christians do not believe in a literal devil. Instead, they believe he is a biblical symbol for evil. But that is not the position of the Bible. The devil is every bit as literal as God is. It's hard for a "symbol" to do the things attributed to Satan in Scripture: deceiving, murdering, tempting, destroying, lying, accusing, and controlling.

In the famous exchange between God and Satan in Job 1, God asked Satan from where he had come. The devil's answer was, "From going to and fro on the earth, and from walking back and forth on it" (Job 1:7). Satan is active on the earth today, involved in human affairs. In fact, the whole world is under his control (1 John 5:19). God has given Satan authority on the earth for a while and will one day take it back; but anyone living on planet Earth at present is subject to the devil's actions. And we must keep our guard up against him.

In the book, *The Art of War*, written twenty-six hundred years ago, author Sun Tzu observed:

> If you know the enemy and know yourself, you need not fear the result of a hundred battles. If you know yourself but not the enemy, for every victory gained you will also suffer a defeat. If you know neither the enemy nor yourself, you will succumb in every battle.[7]

Satan's cleverest strategy is to make us believe that he does not exist.

> **Is it possible for Christians to become preoccupied with the study of Satan and his demons?**

There are two extremes we should avoid. If you hold the position that you don't want to know anything about this subject of the enemy and his forces and you aren't going to study it, then you give Satan an advantage through your ignorance of him. On the other hand, if you think you need to know all there is and you read just about every word in print about Satan, then you don't focus on all the other parts of the Bible that God wants you to dwell on. Know your enemy, but reject the trend to become preoccupied with Satan and his demons.

What do we know about Satan's origin?

Satan's original name was Lucifer, which means "shining one," "morning star," or "son of the morning." And strange as it may sound, he came from heaven. Lucifer was the chief of the cherubim—the highest order of angels. And before the fall, he was in Eden, the garden of God, and had access to the throne of God (Ezekiel 28:13-14).

We also know that Lucifer was full of wisdom and perfect in beauty (Ezekiel 28:12). In fact, Ezekiel 28:13 describes the beauty of Lucifer with gems that reflected the glory of God: "sardius, topaz, and diamond, beryl, onyx, and jasper, sapphire, turquoise, and emerald with gold." No creature had been so fully prepared to reflect the glory of God.

This same passage in Ezekiel also gives us a musical description: "The workmanship of your timbrels and pipes was prepared for you on the day you were created" (verse 13). Satan had been given a very special, very distinctive commission from God to minister unto Him and cover His glory with music through worship and praise. Of Lucifer's musical abilities, Terry Law has written: "Pipes apparently were built into his very body. . . . He was a master musician."[8] He was a walking orchestra. And that was the distinctive, creative purpose that God gave to him. He was one of God's best works of creation for the purpose of praising God in heaven.

From the pomp and beauty of heaven, this glorious creation will be "brought down to Sheol, to the lowest depths of the Pit" (Isaiah 14:15). All his beauty will be gone. In the epic poem *Paradise Lost* by John Milton, we see this illustrated. There is a battle in heaven as Satan and his followers fight for supremacy against God. After being defeated and chained in a lake of fire, Satan is still not willing to accept defeat. Satan would rather be a king in hell than a servant in heaven. So great is Satan's arrogance, that even after being cast out of heaven, he continues to work to subvert the plans of God through corrupting his creation, mankind. In man's eyes he attempts to make evil seem good as he infects mankind with false gods. From the glories of heaven where he was created, his ultimate destination for all eternity will be a "Pit."

What caused Lucifer to fall from heaven?

Lucifer was perfect, "till iniquity was found in [him]" (Ezekiel 28:15). Isaiah 14:13-14 tells us what happened in Lucifer's heart when he rebelled against God:

> For you have said in your heart: "I will ascend into heaven, I will exalt my throne above the stars of God; I will also sit on the mount of the congregation on the farthest sides of the north; I will ascend above the heights of the clouds, I will be like the Most High."

Satan's heart was captivated by pride. He decided it was no longer good enough to be a perfect angel created in the beauty of God. He wanted to be like "the Most High." He desired God's place in heaven—His position, His power, His perfection, His privilege. And when Lucifer became Satan because of the sin of his own heart, he was banished from heaven (Ezekiel 28:16-18). His proud heart was the reason for his fall, and the Bible tells us he did indeed fall. In Jesus' own words, "I saw Satan fall like lightning from heaven" (Luke 10:18).

The essential vice, the utmost evil, is Pride. . . . It was through Pride that the devil became the devil. Pride leads to every other vice. It is the complete anti-God state of mind.[9]

C. S. Lewis

How could a perfect, holy being fall?

Satan wasn't created as the devil. God created Lucifer; and Lucifer became Satan of his own will. But how? Satan had no sinful world to lure him, no tempter to push him, and no innate sinful nature to overpower him. How could the first unholy affection arise in an angelic being? The answer lies in the fact that Lucifer was created with a freedom to choose, just as we were created. Each of us has full choice—the opportunity to say "yes" to God. Lucifer chose to use his gift against the Giver. In his own heart, he determined that he would lift himself up in pride. And that was the first sin ever committed in the universe—the sin of pride.

Because of his anointed role in the heavenlies and his great beauty, Lucifer's heart was lifted up in pride and he was cast out of heaven by God (Ezekiel 28:17). To this day Satan remains a creature filled with arrogance, pride, and rebellion against God (Isaiah 14:12-14). It is a warning to us as Christians that since Satan's personality is characterized by pride, that he would tempt us by using the same weakness in ourselves.

> "It was pride that
> changed angels into devils;
> it is humility that makes
> men as angels."
> *Augustine*

What names are given to Satan in the Bible?

If you read through the Bible and you underline the names for Satan (you might call them the "nicknames"), you will discover a lot about him.

Here is kind of a summary list of some names that are given to Satan in the Bible:

Your adversary (1 Peter 5:8)

. . . the accuser of our brethren (Revelation 12:10)

. . . an angel of light (2 Corinthians 11:14)

. . . the deceiver (Revelation 12:9)

. . . the destroyer (Revelation 9:11)

. . . the evil one (John 17:15)

. . . liar (John 8:44)

. . . a murderer (John 8:44)

. . . the prince of the power of the air (Ephesians 2:2)

. . . the ruler of this world (John 12:31, 14:30, 16:11)

. . . the serpent (Genesis 3:4; Revelation 20:2)

. . . the tempter (Matthew 4:3).

There are many names for Satan in the Bible, and all of them describe him as our enemy.

Does Satan have his own kingdom?

Many theologians believe that when Satan rebelled, one-third of the angels in heaven rebelled with him, came to earth, and now comprise his army of rebellion against God (Revelation 12:4). Satan is not alone in his evil pursuits; he is the head of his own kingdom (Matthew 12:26). He has hierarchies of principalities, and powers, and angels, and demons; and he rules it all. Three times the Bible calls Satan "the prince of this world" (John 12:31; John 14:30; John 16:11, NIV). He's also called "the prince of the power of the air" (Ephesians 2:2). As the prince of this world, he's in charge of evil men; and as the prince of the power of the air, he's in charge of evil spirits. He is defined as both a roaring lion and a great dragon and is described as diabolical, deceptive, destructive, rebellious, and filled with hate.

Satan is the second most powerful person in the universe, subject only to God. The Bible says that men are held captive by that power until delivered by the power of the Savior.

Is Satan's army organized?

It is clear in Scripture that Satan is in control of and commands a great army of fallen angels. In the force of evil that is described in Ephesians 6:12, we are told that his army is organized, that there is a hierarchy in the domain of Satan:

> For we do not wrestle against flesh and blood, but against principalities, against powers, against the rulers of the darkness of this age, against spiritual *hosts* of wickedness in the heavenly *places*.

In the Greek language, the *principalities* refer to the "first" or the "head officers." The *powers* that are mentioned here have to do with staff officers. The *rulers* are divisional commanders. And with this rank and file is the spiritual host of wickedness. In other words, there is an organized effort on the part of Satan to do his work in the world. He has charted the world and organized it, and we are part of his organized plan.

The great trouble with the world today and with the church unfortunately, is that they know so little about the devil and his "principalities and powers."[10]

D. Martyn Lloyd-Jones

Is Satan a god?

The Bible says, strange as it may be, that Satan is a god—with a lowercase "g." Second Corinthians 4:4 says it this way: ". . . whose minds the god of this age has blinded." Who is the god of this age? It is Satan.

Satan is the founder and president of his own religion. He has his own church (Revelation 2:9; 3:9). He has his own gospel (Galatians 1:8). He has his own ministers (2 Corinthians 11:15). He has his own doctrine (1 Timothy 4:1). And he has his own communion table and his own cup (1 Corinthians 10:20-21).

He is the god of this age.

How powerful is Satan?

In 2 Thessalonians 2:9 we read that the workings of Satan come with all power, and signs, and lying wonders—so we know he has supernatural power. First Peter 5:8 describes Satan as a roaring, devouring lion. He is deceptive. He is seductive. He is destructive. And he is filled with hatred. He has his own armor. He has his own strongholds. He has his own strong men. And he is the power behind the world system. First John 5:19 says: "The whole world lies under the sway of the wicked one." So Satan definitely has power—power which, apart from our relationship with Christ, we should fear. But as Christians, we can stand firm on the battlefield because greater is He who lives in us than Satan who lives in the world (1 John 4:4).

The Bible tells us that God has Satan on a leash (Job 1-2). He may have a little power in this day, which has been granted to him under the sovereignty of God; but one day, he will be confined forever in the lake of fire with his angels. We have the victory through Christ. Satan's power is power under control.

Is Satan God's opposite?

We must never underestimate Satan's power. But we also cannot make the opposite error of believing that Satan is as powerful as Almighty God. Satan is not and never will be all-knowing and all-powerful. He is not the opposite of God. How did Satan get here in the first place? He is God's creation. So don't be tempted to think, *God's over here and He's all-powerful for good; and Satan's over here and he's all-powerful for evil.* That's not true. Satan is no match for God. God has no opposite.

How does Satan attempt to deceive the world?

Spiritual deception may be Satan's most insidious weapon in his guerrilla warfare against us. Jesus and the apostles speak of it nearly thirty times in the New Testament. John 8:44 records Jesus' reply to a group of Jews who were resisting His message. Jesus boldly told them that they were children of their father the devil, and that they were not hearing the truth because their father's native language was lies. A person's native language is what he converses in most easily. And Satan speaks the language of deception most fluently.

Revelation 12:9 refers to Satan as the one "who deceives the whole world," which he does by imitating the work of God with counterfeit and camouflage. In fact, Satan's last and greatest deception will be to bring the Antichrist to the world at the end of the age. The Antichrist will initially be a peacemaker who uses persuasive speech and manifests supernatural powers much as the real Christ did. But once people fall for this counterfeit, the Antichrist will lead people not to God, but away from Him.

Pastor and theologian R. Kent Hughes explains one of the reasons for Satan's effectiveness as a deceiver and manipulator:

> I am no genius at mathematics, but even with my limited capabilities I could be terrific at math if I worked on it for 100 years (maybe!). If I labored at it for 1,000 years and read all the learned theories, I would be a Newton or an Einstein. Or what if I had 10,000 years? Given that time, any of us could become the world's great philosopher or psychologist or theologian or linguist … Satan has had a millennia to study and master the human disciplines, and when it comes to human subversion, he is the ultimate manipulator.[11]

The devil's incognitos are very clever. He hides in the most unbelievable places. He hides in religion, one of his favorite hideouts. He hides behind intellectualism. He hides in poetry and art and oftentimes in music. He hides in psychology and human understanding. Satan can even use the subtle method of Scripture taken out of context to deceive many. When people take verses out of their context and use them to prove something they were not intended to prove, they're falling right into the lap of Satan.

Satan never comes out with blatant error—that would be too easily discerned. And that is why we as the people of God must stay alert.

How does Satan attempt to imitate God?

Here's the part about Satan's deception that most people don't realize: he is the great counterfeiter and the great mimic. Satan himself said, "I will be like the Most High" (Isaiah 14:14). And when you watch Satan work in the world, you will begin to notice that everything the Lord has done, Satan attempts to duplicate.

Jesus is the Prince of Peace (Isaiah 9:6); Satan is the prince of the world (John 12:31; 14:30; 16:11, NIV). Jesus is the light of the world (John 9:5); Satan is transformed into an angel of light (2 Corinthians 11:14). Jesus Christ is "the Lord my God" (Zechariah 14:5); Satan is the god of this age (2 Corinthians 4:4). Jesus is "the Lion of the tribe of Judah" (Revelation 5:5); Satan is a roaring lion, seeking whom he may devour (1 Peter 5:8).

Satan tries to do everything God does, because he wants to be like God.

How does Satan stir division in the body of Christ?

I have heard many stories of churches where there's been a great division, where there's been a great split and things have happened that have destroyed the peace and unity of the body of Christ. Let me tell you who's behind all of that—Satan himself.

Satan likes to use the time-honored strategy of divide and conquer. When he was cast out of heaven, he took a third of the angels with him. He divided the first human family, pitting Cain against Abel. He tempted Ananias and Sapphira to divide their loyalty between God and money. And today, Satan is up to the same strategy. He continues to bring division to friendships, fellowships, small groups, churches, and church staff. How? He injects the poisons of suspicion and intolerance and hatred and jealousy and criticism—poisons that seek an outlet. Oftentimes that outlet is the human tongue—our words. James says the tongue "is set on fire by hell . . . . It is an unruly evil, full of deadly poison" (James 3:6, 8). And when we find words hurting and dividing, guess who is delighted in those situations? Wherever you see Satan at work, you'll find division.

Descriptions of Satan in the Bible

 He is a **serpent** trying to deceive God's people.
- Genesis 3:1
- Revelation 12:9

 He is a **bird** trying to despoil God's harvest.
- Matthew 13:4, 19

 He is a **wolf** trying to defeat God's flock.
- John 10:12
- Matthew 10:16

 He is a **lion** trying to devour God's children.
- 1 Peter 5:8

 He is a **dragon** trying to destroy God's Son.
- Revelation 12:1-9

How does Satan use the strategy of destruction?

In Revelation 9:11, the apostle John calls Satan "Apollyon," which in the Greek means "destroyer." That name really suits the devil, doesn't it? Satan will do anything to destroy, delay, demolish, or dismantle God's work. Job, from the Old Testament, is a prime example. When Satan was given access to Job, he destroyed everything (including Job's health) except Job and his wife—he even destroyed Job's wife's attitude toward her husband. Fortunately, Job resisted and kept the faith and saw God bless him richly at the end of his test.

Satan knows he can't destroy God, so his next tactic is to destroy the people of God—to cause adversity in our lives. And he will take any opportunity, however small and seemingly insignificant, to destroy a lifetime of faithfulness to God. So stay on guard!

How does Satan use the strategy of distraction?

The idea of staging an intervention in a person's life to arrest the progress of some kind of injurious or unwise behavior is well known. The goal is to intervene—to break the normal cycle of behavior and substitute clinical help or other better behaviors. Just so, Satan loves to intervene in our lives to do just the opposite: distract us from our healthy spiritual behaviors and tempt us with bad behaviors. If he can distract us from the spiritually productive priorities in our life and occupy us with the things of this world, his intervention will be successful. If we are too busy to pray, study the Bible, serve others, attend church or Bible studies, then we will not grow spiritually. We will remain babes in Christ. There's nothing wrong with being busy, of course, as long as we are busy with the right things and we don't get so busy that we begin to think of our busyness as a way of impressing God. Even that is a trap of Satan to distract us from true spirituality.

What are the "wiles of the devil"?

The Bible teaches us that Satan is attacking the lives and causes that would defeat his plans. That is why all of us who are Christians feel so much of the effect of Satan's presence. He is not after those who belong to him. Satan concentrates his efforts on those who want to defeat him. That's his purpose: to drown the influence of men and women who claim to know Jesus Christ. And the Bible says Satan has a method for doing this. We're doing battle in life today against "the wiles of the devil" (Ephesians 6:11).

Now, *wiles* is not a word we use a lot in our culture today. It means "organized conduct, plans of war or strategy or methodology." And I personally believe that Satan has a strategy for every one of us. He knows our weaknesses; he knows our strengths. And he will stop at nothing if he thinks he can victimize us for his own purposes.

The Greek word *methodeia* is translated as "wiles" or "wile" in the King James Version from the English word *method*. This is another indication that the one who is planning to attack us is organized and systematic. Those are the "wiles of the devil" we must guard against.

What are some ways we give ground to the enemy?

When we know what is right and we compromise that in our minds in order to indulge something we want to do, we have given ground to the enemy. When we hear the voice of God speaking to us clearly, and for reasons of our comfort, or perhaps even out of fear, we postpone our obedience, we open up the door for the enemy to make an attack upon us.

The Bible says that the devil, as a roaring lion, goes about seeking whom he may devour. He wants to so change who we are that we no longer have any power of commitment or testimony. He wants us to fall into fleshly things that destroy our ability to stand for the Lord. That's what he's seeking to do. Satan wants, primarily, to devour our influence for Christ. And when we run from the enemy, we open ourselves up to ultimate defeat. Don't give Satan an opportunity to come along your flank and destroy you. Don't turn away from him. Rather, keep him in view, and stand strong in the midst of his attempts to destroy.

Are demons real?

While there are some today who deny the reality of demons, the Bible gives abundant evidence for their existence. More than eighty times in the New Testament, we are introduced to demons; and in most cases, it is in relationship to the Lord Jesus Christ Himself. Christ believed in the reality of demons, and He demonstrated His power over them often:

- "At evening, when the sun had set, they brought to Him all who were sick and those who were demon-possessed" (Mark 1:32).

- "And He was preaching in their synagogues throughout all Galilee, and casting out demons" (Mark 1:39).

- "Then His fame went throughout all Syria; and they brought to Him all sick people who were afflicted with various diseases

and torments, and those who were demon-
possessed, epileptics, and paralytics; and
He healed them"
(Matthew 4:24).

- "And that very hour He cured many of
  infirmities, afflictions, and evil spirits; and
  to many blind He gave sight"
  (Luke 7:21).

Satan is not alone in his spiritual attacks.

Jesus speaks of the eternal fire prepared "for the
devil *and his angels*" (Matthew 25:41). Satan "*and his
angels*" are referred to together in Revelation 12:9. In
Matthew 12:24 he is called "Beelzebub, the ruler *of
the demons*."

These spirits are rational beings, not diseases or
ailments, or tricks of the imagination. They possess
all the attributes of personality. They even believe
in God, as James tells us "You believe that there is
one God. Good! Even *the demons believe* that—and
shudder" (2:19, NIV). Demons think and believe and
hear and speak.

What are demons?

Demons are Satan's servants, and are committed to his scheme to thwart the plan of God. Often in Scripture they are also called "evil spirits" or "unclean spirits." They are ruled by Satan himself, and they share in his dirty work.

With enemies like these, we need friends. God has provided them, and shows them to us in His Word.

Lock on to the fact that nothing demons do can be outside God's good purpose and design. Never forget this: "Neither angels *nor demons … nor any powers* … nor anything else in all creation, will be able to separate us from the love of God that is in Christ Jesus our Lord" (Romans 8:38-39, NIV).

John Calvin provided a thoughtful illustration of this thought. He described God "turning the unclean spirits hither and thither at his pleasure," all with the intention of "exercising believers." The demons are always "warring against them, assailing them with wiles, urging them with solicitations, pressing close upon them, disturbing, alarming, and occasionally wounding, but *never conquering or oppressing them.*"

Just as Satan and the demons share a common origin and a common passion and work, so they also must face a common fate. Paul assures us that Jesus "must reign until he has put *all his enemies* under his feet" (1 Corinthians 15:25, NIV). This includes the devil and every demon.

Are there different kinds of demons?

When we study the Bible, there are two kinds of demons that we learn about. There are what we might call "the fallen and the free" and "the fallen and the imprisoned."

"The fallen and the free" are those demons who are creating all the havoc and stress in the world today under Satan's control. Then there are "the fallen and the imprisoned"—a class of demons who are already imprisoned in a place called *Tartarus*, one of the compartments of hell. Jude 1:6 says, "And the angels who did not keep their proper domain, but left their own abode, He has reserved in everlasting chains under darkness for the judgment of the great day." And they will be there forever and ever. They will never get out. And the Scripture says it's because they "did not keep their proper domain."

In Genesis we read that when the fallen angels saw the daughters of men, they were filled with lust and cohabited with them, bearing offspring which were half angelic and half human—a superhuman product called in biblical language, the *nephilim*, meaning "giant" (Genesis 6:1-2, 4). This violation of God-given boundaries so grieved God that He decided immediately to send a flood to destroy the whole earth, saving only eight souls alive through the ark. And it was because of that sin, when the angels left their proper domain and entered into the realm of human flesh, that those fallen angels were cast down to hell "into chains of darkness, to be reserved for judgment" (2 Peter 2:4).

In every encounter between Jesus and demons in the Gospels, Jesus was the overcomer. His followers share in that power. When Christ's disciples returned "with joy" from a ministry trip, they reported to Jesus, "Lord, even *the demons submit to us* in your name" (Luke 10:17, NIV). And Jesus answers, "*I saw Satan fall* like lightning from heaven" (Luke 10:18, NIV).

Jude says that God has kept the fallen angels "in darkness, *bound with everlasting chains* for judgment on the great Day" (Jude 6, NIV).

Meanwhile, until that great Day, we wrestle. We "*struggle* ... against the powers of this dark world and against the spiritual forces of evil in the heavenly realms" (Ephesians 6:12, NIV).

In this struggle there is someone who shows us how to endure and how to win, someone whose life knew more spiritual warfare than anyone who ever walked the earth. That Someone is Jesus.

Can a believer be possessed by a demon?

Demons are actively involved in the world today. But I believe the Bible is clear that Christians cannot be demon-possessed. First Corinthians 6:19 says, "Or do you not know that your body is the temple of the Holy Spirit *who is* in you, whom you have from God, and you are not your own?" Believers are permanently indwelt by the Spirit of God. And in 1 John 4:4 we read, "You are of God, little children, and have overcome them, because He who is in you is greater than he who is in the world." He who is in us is the Holy Spirit; and he who is in the world is Satan with his demons. And the conclusion is quite clear—a demon is not able to enter and take control of a believer because the Holy Spirit is stronger than any demonic being, including Satan himself. It's that simple.

Christians are troubled by the devil, tempted by the devil, and perhaps even obsessed with the devil, but never possessed by him.

What will ultimately happen to Satan and his army of fallen angels?

The devil and his demons are doomed to everlasting punishment. There is no hope for them because Jesus Christ did not shed His blood on Calvary to redeem the fallen angels. They fell from the level of perfection, living in the presence of God Almighty as His chosen cherubs of worship. Of their own volition, out of their own desire, they rebelled against God.

One day, Satan will be cast into the bottomless pit for 1,000 years, and then he will be thrown into the lake of fire along with his angels. God has already won the victory over Satan and his army. Their judgment is sure (Matthew 25:41). We are just waiting for the day when the sentence will be carried out in complete detail.

> "Then He will also say to those on the left hand, 'Depart from Me, you cursed, into the everlasting fire prepared for the devil and his angels.'"
> *Matthew 25:41*

*God's
Armory*

Stand therefore,
having girded your waist
with truth, having put on the
breastplate of righteousness,
and having shod your feet with
the preparation of the gospel
of peace; above all, taking the
shield of faith with which you
will be able to quench all the
fiery darts of the wicked one.
And take the helmet of salvation,
and the sword of the Spirit,
which is the word of God.

Ephesians 6:14-17

What armor has God given me for warfare?

This war is not one that we have to go into unprotected. There are six pieces of spiritual armor mentioned by the apostle Paul in Ephesians 6:14-17, each dealing with a specific area of our life.

1. The Girdle of Truth

2. The Breastplate of Righteousness

3. The Shoes of the Gospel of Peace

4. The Shield of Faith

5. The Helmet of Salvation

6. The Sword of the Spirit

Don't be a casualty of spiritual warfare. Get in the battle and defeat the enemy by wearing the full armor of God!

THE GIRDLE OF TRUTH

Stand therefore, having girded
your waist with truth.
Ephesians 6:14

What protection does the girdle of truth provide?

Paul first tells us to be girded about with truth, referring to the belt that harnessed the soldier's weapons to his body. Today's well-dressed soldiers are outfitted with a combat harness, a modern version of the Roman soldier's belt but which serve the same function. It allows them to carry all their needed equipment in a confined space under combat conditions. This harness includes pouches for extra ammo, grenades, a canteen, a radio or satellite phone, and other items such as medical provisions or personal supplies.

For the Christian, this combat harness is *truth*. Paul said, *Stand therefore, having girded your waist with truth.* This is important because of the nature of our enemy. Satan is determined to hinder and harm God's work in our lives. He is here to steal, to kill, and to destroy. He's like a roaring lion seeking someone to destroy. He is a liar from the beginning, a deceiver, a serpent. He is the accuser of the brethren. Whatever he says to us is a distortion.

The historian William Manchester, in his two-volume biography of Winston Churchill, said that Churchill "adopted, as a working thesis, the assumption that any given foreign policy statement by Hitler was the exact opposite of truth." It was an assumption that served Churchill well, for Hitler was a liar and deceiver from the beginning.

We can make the same assumption about the devil. John 8 says that Satan is a liar, and there is no truth in him. He comes at us with deception, sham, trickery, and falsity. He wants to entangle us. Notice how he has blurred the values of right and wrong in our society. Notice how his propaganda machine—today's mass entertainment media—glorifies immorality while ridiculing biblical values.

That means that Christians must be children of truth. We have to implement truth in our lives. Jesus said, "I am the ... truth" (John 14:6). John 1:14 says that He was "full of grace and truth." Jesus said that God's Word was truth (John 17:17). He told His disciple: "If you abide in My Word, you are My disciples indeed. And you shall know the truth, and the truth shall make you free" (John 8:31-32).

How do I arm myself with the girdle of truth?

In order to be armed with the truth, we must know the truth—the whole comprehensive counsel of God. God has put everything He wants us to know between the covers of the Bible—everything He wants us to know about Himself, about His Son, about eternity, and about life. And when we study God's Word, carefully analyze and apply its truth, we end up with power in our lives.

Now, you might never memorize the whole Bible, but make it a priority to know your Bible well enough to know that there are certain places in Scripture where you are going to find answers. The more truth we know, the better equipped we are to go into battle and be victorious. And when you take God's truth to yourself, then you can embody that truth in your life, and God will begin to show you how you can be victorious on the battlefield.

How can I discern Satan's lies from truth?

Someone once told me that if you want to identify a crooked stick, the best thing you can do is lay a straight stick down next to it. That same principle works when dealing with the deceit of Satan. If you will lay the "straight stick" of God's Word next to what it is you are trying to discern, you will usually be able to identify Satan's deceitful propaganda.

But I recently read an article written by Roger Olson, in which he recommends an additional tool. He wrote:

> I believe it is important and valuable for Christians to know not only theological correctness (orthodoxy) but also the ideas of those judged as heretics within the church's story. One reason is that it is almost impossible to appreciate the meaning of orthodoxy without under-standing the heresies that forced its development.[12]

The apostle Paul warns that Satan takes advantage of us when we are ignorant of his strategies (2 Corinthians 2:11).

What does it mean to live a life of truthfulness?

Truth is objective. It's there. It's true or it's not true. But truthfulness is somewhat subjective. Truthfulness is whether or not the truth we have about God has caused us to be people who are truthful.

If we want to be warriors in the battle against Satan, we have to have integrity and sincerity. Third John 1:4 says, "I have no greater joy than to hear that my children walk in truth." In other words, they don't just know the truth, they're living a life of truthfulness. Such a walk implies that we are dealing with the realities of life with sin and with ourselves; we're not allowing any conscious hypocrisy or any excuse or condoning sin. That means we're seeking to be honest before the Lord and before others; we're not faking the Christian life and putting a spin on what it means to be a Christian. That's what the girdle of truth is all about. It's knowing the truth and then allowing that truth to change who we are from the inside out. After all, how can we have any influence in the lives of others about the truth if we're not living the truth in our own life?

Search me, O God, and
know my heart; try me,
and know my anxieties;
and see if *there is any*
wicked way in me,
and lead me in the
way everlasting.

Psalm 139:23-24

What is the importance of a clear conscience?

It is not uncommon to hear someone being instructed to "let their conscience be their guide." But this is not always good advice. It is possible to follow one's conscience and do the wrong thing.

Six times in his pastoral epistles, Paul mentions the conscience. He writes about a good conscience, a pure conscience, and he says that it is possible to have one's conscience "corrupted" (Titus 1:15), or defiled; he describes it as having it "seared with a hot iron…" (1 Timothy 4:2). The writer of Hebrews actually speaks of an "evil conscience" (Hebrews 10:22).

The conscience is a part of our God-given internal faculties, a critical witness within us that tells us we ought to do what we believe to be right and not to do what we believe to be wrong. The conscience does not instruct us as to what is right or wrong but prods us to do what we have been taught is right or wrong.

It is possible to be led astray by our conscience when we are deceived as to what is right and wrong. It is important to understand that our conscience must be informed by the Word of God...what it says is right and what it says is wrong. Without the absolute standard of God's Word, our conscience is an unreliable guide because it is subject to emotions and moods.

D. Martyn Lloyd-Jones makes the observation that present-day religion far too often soothes the conscience instead of awakening it, and produces a sense of self-satisfaction and eternal safety rather than a sense of our unworthiness.

Paul urged Timothy to hold "on to faith and a good conscience" (1 Timothy 1:19, NIV). And he told his young protégé that a deacon in the church should be one who held the "mystery of the faith with a pure conscience" (1 Timothy 3:9).

If we want our conscience to be our ally in holy living, we must saturate it with God's Word and ask the Holy Spirit to convict us of sin and lead us in righteousness. (Acts 23:1, 24:16; Romans 2:15, 9:1; 2 Corinthians 1:12; Hebrews 10:22, 13:18; 1 Peter 2:19, 3:16, 21).

THE BREASTPLATE OF RIGHTEOUSNESS

Put on the breastplate of righteousness.

Ephesians 6:14

What protection does the breastplate of righteousness provide?

Recently, the American Forces Press told of a soldier with the Army's 10th Mountain Division who was knocked down by small arms fire, but who got up and continued his mission. Hit again by enemy fire, the infantryman got up a second time and continued his mission. "He's still alive," said the news report, "thanks to the new Interceptor body armor being worn by soldiers and Marines." It weighs just sixteen pounds, compared to twenty-five pounds for the flak jacket, the previous body armor. Engineers are working to create an even lighter, stronger vest. "Our goal is to create a protective system that is lower profile, lower bulk and lower weight," said one inventor. "We want it to be like a second skin, so the warfighter barely even knows that it's there, but that offers the protections needed in a combat environment."

When Paul said the well-dressed Christian soldier must wear the "breastplate of righteousness," he meant that the righteousness of Christ should be like our "second skin." It will protect us from being trapped and defeated.

In one sense, of course, Christians are already equipped with the righteousness of Christ. We call this *positional* righteousness. According to 1 Corinthians 1:30, Christ *became* our righteousness, and when we trust Him as Savior, we are clothed in Him. When God sees us, He doesn't see us in our sins; He sees us clothed in the righteousness of Christ. That is our position before God.

But we must practice *practical* righteousness. We must commit ourselves to a life that is honest, upright, authentic, and full of integrity. When we find little ways of lying, cheating, and shading the truth, we give Satan a foothold. Nothing so demoralizes and discourages a warrior as being involved in a spiritual battle, knowing there is a problem of character and integrity in his own life. The little sins we tolerate represent dangerous "holes" in our bulletproof vests. You can be sure that sooner or later, Satan will aim right at that spot.

We're in a battle, and our enemy is on the attack. We need to resist him. Satan can't stand the hymns of the faith, so sing. He can't overcome the prayers of the saints, so pray. He can't defeat the Lord Jesus Christ, so claim the power of the Blood. He can't overthrow the truth, so quote the Scriptures. He can't vanquish the joy of the Lord, so rejoice. He can't divert God's grace, so use the shield of faith.

We must use the weapons God has given us. Resist the devil and he will flee from you. Draw near to God and He will draw near to you.

> It may be that Satan is planning some fresh temptation with which to assail you; but, though he desires to … sift you as wheat, Christ is praying for you, that your faith fail not.
> *Charles H. Spurgeon,* in his sermon "The Tenses"

What is the importance of righteousness in battle?

There is no power in a Christian's life if it is not a righteous life. Apart from righteousness, we really have no defense against Satan's accusations. And every time we try to do battle with the enemy, he will go right for that weakness and bring to mind the sin in our life and perhaps even make us doubt our salvation. We won't witness because we'll think, *How can I tell them what Christ has done for me when my life is not any different than theirs?* Neither will we be victorious over temptation. Without righteousness, we are powerless to withstand Satan's tactics. But the Christian who is wearing the breastplate of righteousness will go through life and, no matter what happens, find some victory in every situation. In times of stress, in times of joy, in rejoicing, in sorrow, in plenty, in want, there will be a consistent quality about his life. That's what happens when you have the righteousness of Christ in you and when you are outwardly living the righteousness of Christ.

What is sanctification?

The word "sanctification" means "to be set apart for a specific purpose." It is another way of looking at our journey with Christ and it comes in three tenses—three dramatic dimensions. *Past sanctification* is the moment when we say yes to Christ, are sealed by the Holy Spirit, and have our sins washed by the blood of Christ, with that debt declared paid in full, so that we are seated with Him in the heavenly places. And that's just the past part.

Present sanctification is an ongoing growth process, as spiritual molecule by spiritual molecule we are conformed to the image of Christ through the redeeming work of the Holy Spirit. Through prayer and the Word, we learn to experience victory in Christ, issue by issue.

Then, most thrilling of all, there is a *future sanctification*. There will be a day when we are finally freed from the presence of sin. As there can be no sin in heaven, no impurity in God's holy presence, it must finally be eliminated for good. We will see that happen, and I can't imagine how wonderful it will be. The best definition I've ever heard for *sanctification* is this: "Becoming in practice what you already are in position." And what are Christians "in position"? We are clothed in the righteousness of Christ. Sanctification is the process of growing in holiness—living every day in light of who we are in Christ.

This is threefold sanctification. It began when I trusted Christ, and the penalty was removed. It continued as I began walking with the Lord, and more and more I learned how to be victorious over temptation and in trials. Sanctification will be complete when Jesus takes me unto Himself in the future, when sin is judged and destroyed, and eternal life begins for us. And that day, Paul tells us, "is nearer than when we first believed" (Romans 13:11).

> In the way of righteousness *is* life, and in its pathway *there is* no death.
>
> *Proverbs 12:28*

How can I be consistent in righteousness?

The Bible teaches us that we're to cultivate righteousness in our lives until, like a habit, it becomes an automatic part of who we are. And I've had many Christians over the years tell me they get discouraged because they fail. Their Christian life is like a yo-yo, up and down, up and down. The question then is, "How can I be righteous? Can I try harder?" Apparently, the apostle Paul attempted that approach. He decided to try harder, but he failed when he tried to do it in his own strength (Romans 7:15, 19). Someone might say, "Well then, should I just give it up to God?" But how does that work? How can we become righteous by just passively waiting for it to happen to us? No, the answer doesn't lie in either one of those strategies. Instead of trying to live better, we need to learn how to love better. We need to fall more deeply in love with God, because that relationship will dictate our conduct. When we learn how to love the Lord through His Word and through prayer and fellowship and worship . . . when we practice the art of holiness . . . when we take time to be holy and love God with all our heart . . . it will change our life.

How can I know my heart is right?

The Bible tells us that "where [our] treasure is, there [our] heart will be also" (Matthew 6:21). What this means is that our heart dictates our lifestyle and defines our priorities. Sometimes people wonder, *Can I do this? Can I get by with doing this or that?* But when we have thoughts like these, we are often just asking, *How close can I get to the things of the world without getting in trouble with God?* And when we do that, we are giving away our affection. When you really love somebody, you don't try to live as far away from them as you can. You do everything possible to live as close to them as you can. This is the nature of love. Unfortunately, there are churches that have fostered the idea that when you become a Christian, you "give up" the things of the world. But be assured, when you are pursuing the righteousness of Christ, you begin to realize that you're uncomfortable with some of the things that are going on in your life; and when you walk away from those things, you won't miss them, because God replaces them with something far better.

THE SHOES OF
THE GOSPEL OF PEACE

Shod your feet with the preparation
of the gospel of peace.
Ephesians 6:15

What protection do the shoes of the gospel of peace provide?

The Romans wore special shoes for warfare—thick-soled, hobnailed sandals with thick leather straps. These sandals provided better traction for battle and gave soldiers a foundation that would protect their feet from injury and traps set by the enemy. So why does Paul say Christians should put on the shoes of the gospel of peace? As soldiers of Christ, we too must have a good foundation for warfare— "the preparation of the gospel of peace." The word *preparation* comes from a Greek word which means "readiness" or "firmness." We must stand firm and trust that the One who has called us into battle will always be working for our good. If we spend our time worrying and fretting or questioning God's care and concern for us, we will be unproductive on the battlefield (Matthew 6:26-27). The gospel of peace stabilizes our hearts because we know that God is on our side! He is working for our good! And the settled peace that only He can provide is our foundation for fighting.

How do I arm myself with the shoes of the gospel of peace?

We're not primarily in a battle against people, but against the realm of devilish powers; so it's important to be equipped with the inward peace produced by the Gospel of Christ. Paul had previously said in Ephesians 2:14 that Christ is our peace. Jesus comes to us in the midst of the battle, when the struggle against temptation or the discouragements of life seem impossible, and He speaks peace to us. He gives the encouragement that keeps our morale up. That is the foundation on which we must fight—the shoes of peace.

How can we minister to others in this world of woe and warfare if our own hearts are so upset that we seem no different than anyone else? It's like going into battle barefoot, grimacing in pain as the rocks of anxiety press into our tender soles. Just as the right boots protect our soles, the peace of the Gospel protects our souls. The Good News of Christ brings composure to our lives. It puts hard leather between us and the jagged stones of fear and doubt.

That's why the Bible constantly tells us, "Do not fret … do not fear … do not let your hearts be troubled … do not be anxious … don't be discouraged." Are you going into your daily warfare shod with divine peace?

A great method to help you requisition this peace in your life is Scripture memory. After all, Scripture is the Word of Peace. And when you get the Word of God in your life, you will find help to deal with the inevitable problems and stresses of life.

> "You will keep him in perfect peace, whose mind is stayed on You, because he trusts in You."
> *Isaiah 26:3*

We gradually grow in our
ability to experience
the peace of God as
we grow in Christ.

What does it mean to let the peace of God "rule" in my heart?

Colossians 3:15 says we are to "let the peace of God rule in [our] hearts." In the language of the New Testament, the word *rule* is a word meaning "umpire." In other words, let the peace of God umpire your heart.

When you have a decision to make and you're walking with the Lord, one of the ways that you test your decision is by whether or not the Lord gives you peace about that decision. Have you ever heard someone say, "You know, I'd like to do this, but I just don't have peace about it"? I believe that God uses that sense of peace in our hearts to confirm and direct our decisions. That's how He rules in our hearts. When you put on the shoes of peace, measure your life by the rule of peace, and let that rule make a difference in your life.

> And the peace of God, which surpasses all understanding, will guard your hearts and minds through Christ Jesus.
> *Philippians 4:7*

Peace I leave with you,
My peace I give to you;
not as the world gives
do I give to you. Let not
your heart be troubled.

John 14:27

THE SHIELD OF FAITH

Above all, [take] the shield of faith
with which you will be able to quench
all the fiery darts of the wicked one.
Ephesians 6:16

What protection does the shield of faith provide?

Roman battle shields were about four feet tall and two feet wide. The shields were covered with thick leather and metal so as to deflect incoming arrows, which were often tipped with leather and dipped in fiery pitch. The shield protected the soldiers from these flying, fiery darts. For the Christian, that shield is faith. In fact, faith is the key to all spiritual armor. And it is given to us to deflect the fiery darts of Satan—darts that have but one purpose, and that is to produce doubt, distress of mind, depression of spirit, and disappointment in relationships or in work or in yourself. The shield of our faith in Christ is our defense (Psalm 18:30; Proverbs 30:5; 1 John 5:4). And Scripture promises us that this shield is sufficient to repel even the enemy's best shot. Without that defense we become very vulnerable; because Satan knows what armor we have and he knows where the joints, or cracks, are between our armor. That's where he aims. Without the shield of faith, Satan can take us out. So, the Bible says, "Above all, don't forget the shield!" It is a priority.

Reverend J. O. Fraser, missionary to the Lisu people in China, labored on the China/Burma border for a number of years with no apparent success. Many men would have given up; but when discouraged, Fraser simply prayed and trusted—and kept working.

Here's what he wrote in his journal on January 16, 1916, "Not a single person at service in the morning … The walls of Jericho fell down 'by faith.' Of all the instances of faith in Hebrews 11, this corresponds most nearly to my case."

Later, on February 5 after a day of fighting

off the devil's darts of discouragement, he wrote: "I am not taking the black, despondent view I took yesterday. The opposition will not be overcome be reasoning or by pleading, but (chiefly) by steady, persistent prayer …. I am now setting my face like a flint: if the work seems to fail, then pray; if services, etc., fall flat, then pray still more; if months slip by with little or no result, the pray still more and get others to help you."

Finally the long awaited revival came like a dam-burst; and to this day, the Lisu areas are among the most solidly Christian in China.

Why couldn't Satan defeat Fraser? The missionary held up the shield of faith. First John 5:4 (KJV) says, "This is the victory that overcometh the world, even our faith."

As for God, His way
is perfect; The word
of the LORD is proven;
He *is* a shield to all
who trust in Him.

Psalm 18:30

How do I arm myself with the shield of faith?

In Galatians, Paul writes, "I have been crucified with Christ; it is no longer I who live, but Christ lives in me; and the *life* which I now live in the flesh I live by faith in the Son of God, who loved me and gave Himself for me" (2:20). Notice that Paul does not say, "I live my life in the flesh by *my* faith in the Son of God." No, it's not our faith; it is the faith that God gives us. Even our faith is a gift from God; our faith in Jesus Christ is our shield. And we are to "take up the shield of faith" (Ephesians 6:16, NIV).

Faith has to be appropriated; then it can be used. The way we appropriate faith in our lives is by arming ourselves with the truth about God and who He is so that for every "fiery dart" Satan sends our way, we will have an appropriate answer, an appropriate truth, or an appropriate verse which we can use to repel him. We need to take what God has given us in the precious promises of His Word and mine out of it the truths that will help us live the practical

Christian life with victory. When we know what we believe, we're actively building our shield of faith so that it will be impervious to any attack Satan sends our way.

> Even our faith is a gift from God; our faith in Jesus Christ is our shield. And we are to "take up the shield of faith."
>
> *Ephesians 6:16,* NIV

What are the "fiery darts of the wicked one"?

Sometimes Satan, "the wicked one," attempts to destroy us by direct attack.

Out there in the hinterland, Satan and his demons are shooting fiery darts at God's people. Sometimes Satan comes after us with a dart of discouragement; and sometimes he sends the dart of mistrust, telling us to doubt our own faith. Other times he sends darts of lust, lies, rumors, gossip, jealousies, covetousness—temptations of all sorts. The devil has a whole quiver full of those things, and he sends them our way when we least expect it. He wants to ruin our testimony and destroy our life. But when we are armed with the shield of faith, we are able to quench every dart Satan sends our way.

How can I join forces with other believers?

In Paul's day, Roman soldiers would lock their shields together and hunker down behind them as a defense against a rain of enemy arrows. They would then use the shields as a defensive "wall" as they moved forward. Stu Weber writes: "Do you see the critical point here? This is the shield of faith, which by design, is interlocked with the soldier next to you. This is the shield of faith utilized in community, the community of faith."[13] The interlocking of shields within the Church is a picture of God's people coming together in church and in small groups and home groups to withstand the enemy and help one another—to watch one another's back so that we can be better protected and prepared for the raining darts of the enemy.

For whatever is born
of God overcomes the
world. And this is the
victory that has overcome
the world—our faith.

1 John 5:4

How can I strengthen my faith?

In order to fortify the strength of our faith, we must first focus on the source of our faith. Faith is irrelevant apart from the object of our faith. And our faith is not in faith itself; our faith is in the Lord God and His promises. The writer of the book of Hebrews tells us that we are to look "unto Jesus, the author and finisher of *our* faith" (Hebrews 12:2). We must keep our eyes on Christ, and we must not become lazy! We need to consistently exercise and practice an active faith. God has given us everything we need: the whole curriculum and all the notes. And we practice by taking what we know from the Word of God and putting it into operation. Before we know it, we're putting together a life of obedience to the Word of God. And that is what builds us strong and makes it possible for us to stand against the wiles of the enemy. Take up the shield of faith!

THE HELMET OF SALVATION

Take the helmet of salvation.

Ephesians 6:17

What protection does the helmet of salvation provide?

The Roman soldier's helmet was obviously designed to protect his head; so it is easy to see the parallel helmet of salvation protecting the believer's mind from the attacks of Satan. But the helmet of salvation is more than simply knowing that you're a Christian. That is important, of course, but the helmet of salvation reaches far beyond the simple terms of salvation; it encompasses the whole scope of salvation—past, present, and future.

The enemy is constantly at work trying to wear down our defenses and corrupt our minds with temptation and rationalization and false teaching—anything to confuse our thinking about God and His purposes for our life. Our only defense is to have the benefit of a mind that has lived in and conquered this world—and that is the mind of Christ. When we put on the helmet of salvation, we are putting on the mind of Christ and the wisdom of God. And Christ wants to equip us with His plans, His thoughts, His concepts, His truth, and His revelation. With Him, we can stand victorious in the midst of the fury of attacks that are leveled against us.

A key theme in the New Testament is that spiritual warfare is not fought as earthly wars are fought—"according to the flesh." Rather, "the weapons of our warfare are not carnal but mighty in God for pulling down strongholds, casting down arguments and every high thing that exalts itself against the knowledge of God, *bringing every thought into captivity to the obedience of Christ*" (2 Corinthians 10:3-5, italics added). This is the same idea expressed by Peter: "Always be ready to give a defense to everyone who asks you a reason for the hope that is in you" (1 Peter 3:15). A defense is a well-reasoned answer—using the mind to defeat untruths concerning God and faith in Him.

The mind must be engaged in order to promote and defend the faith. The primary battlefield for spiritual warfare is always the battlefield of the mind where thoughts compete against one another. And our minds must be filled with the biblical defenses of the faith.

How do I arm myself with the helmet of salvation?

I personally believe that the mind is the most fiercely contested battleground in all of spiritual warfare. Our mind has to be guarded every moment to ensure that Satan does not slip in and plant seeds of carnal or sinful thinking. And in order to do that, the Bible says we're to take to ourselves God's helmet, God's wisdom.

How do we get the wisdom of God? Paul says in 1 Corinthians 1:24 that Jesus Christ has become for us the power and wisdom of God. As we put on Jesus Christ, He becomes the wisdom of God to us. Therefore the helmet of salvation is the wisdom of God in Christ. And it's available to every believer through prayer and the reading of God's Word (James 1:5; 2 Timothy 3:15).

If any of you lacks wisdom, let him ask of God, who gives to all liberally and without reproach, and it will be given to him.

James 1:5

What is wisdom?

Some Christians are operating with knowledge instead of wisdom. They know a lot of facts about Christianity, but they lack the wisdom of God. The best definition of wisdom I have found is from the Old Testament scholar Tremper Longman. He wrote:

> Wisdom is a rich concept and is not easily summarized. . . . Wisdom is the skill of living. It is a practical knowledge that helps one know how to act and how to speak in different situations. Wisdom entails the ability to avoid problems, and the skill to handle them when they present themselves. Wisdom includes the ability to interpret other people's speech and writing in order to react correctly to what they are saying to us.[14]

A simpler definition of wisdom is this: "doing the right thing without a precedent." The believer who can respond to an unexpected situation or circumstance in the same way Christ would is someone who has biblical wisdom—the mind of Christ.

When wisdom enters your heart, and knowledge is pleasant to your soul, discretion will preserve you; understanding will keep you.
Proverbs 2:10-11

Happy is the man who finds wisdom, and the man who gains understanding.
Proverbs 3:13

She is more precious than rubies, and all the things you may desire cannot compare with her. Length of days is in her right hand, in her left hand riches and honor. Her ways are ways of pleasantness, and all her paths are peace. She is a tree of life to those who take hold of her, and happy are all who retain her.
Proverbs 3:15-18

For wisdom is better than rubies, and all the things one may desire cannot be compared with her.
Proverbs 8:11

How does the helmet of salvation prepare me for ministry?

When it comes to spiritual warfare, helmets are not optional. In fact, the helmet of salvation is a prerequisite to any kind of ministry because without our helmet, without God's wisdom, we're going to be prone to making a lot of mistakes and poor decisions.

In Acts 6:3 we read about the early church when they were trying to select the very first deacons: "Therefore, brethren, seek out from among you seven men of *good* reputation, full of the Holy Spirit and wisdom, whom we may appoint over this business." In other words, seek out men who are wearing their helmets.

When Paul wrote to Timothy, he reminded young Timothy of the source of his wisdom: "From childhood you have known the Holy Scriptures, which are able to make you wise for salvation through faith which is in Christ Jesus" (2 Timothy 3:15). Do you know why Timothy was prepared to be a servant of God? His grandmother and his mother had taught him the Scriptures. Timothy was wearing his helmet; he knew the Holy Scriptures that were able to make him "wise for salvation." That's what it takes to do the work of God.

> When it comes to spiritual warfare, helmets are not optional.

How can I find hope in the midst of combat?

The helmet of salvation is the promise of hope. First Thessalonians 5:8 says: "But let us who are of the day be sober, putting on the breastplate of faith and love, and *as* a helmet the hope of salvation."

So what is our hope? It's the hope that we have that Christ is ultimately going to resolve this warfare, that one day He's going to come back and set everything straight. We're fighting in a war that, in essence, we have already won. And we don't have to skirmish around in fear of defeat because we know victory is ours in Christ. So, we put on this helmet of salvation, and the helmet of salvation is our hope in Christ.

In 1 Thessalonians 5:8 Paul refines the concept of the "helmet of salvation." There, he says Christians are to put on "as a helmet the hope of salvation." But in Scripture, salvation is not a "hope" as the world uses the term—something we want but are not sure of. Rather, Christian hope is a certainty.

How can I defend myself in a hostile world?

This world is hostile to the things of God. And there is a built-in conflict when a Christian lives in this world. Matthew 10:18-20 is an important passage in this regard:

> You will be brought before governors and kings for My sake, as a testimony to them and to the Gentiles. But when they deliver you up, do not worry about how or what you should speak. For it will be given to you in that hour what you should speak; for it is not you who speak, but the Spirit of your Father who speaks in you.

This passage is not a license for avoiding study, for just opening your mouth and expecting God to fill it. Instead, it is God's promise that when you are thrust into a situation where a word is required of you immediately, the wisdom of God will be given you out of the storehouse of what you have already committed to mind in your study.

Consider the apostles. They spoke far beyond their own natural ability—their wisdom and power often confounded their opponents.

As Christians, we are going to find ourselves on the defensive in this world, and we must be prepared to speak with the wisdom and power of Christ. We must be prepared to give an answer for the hope that lies within us (1 Peter 3:15). And that will only happen if we nurture our minds in Him—if we put on the helmet of salvation.

As Christians, we are going to find ourselves on the defensive in this world, and we must be prepared to speak with the wisdom and power of Christ.

How can I demolish Satan's strongholds in my heart and mind?

A stronghold was a fortress in the ancient world—a place where an enemy became entrenched. In spiritual terms, a stronghold in the life of a Christian is precisely the same thing. It is a place where the enemy is entrenched—an established pattern or habit or concept in our life that does not yet belong to God. And in each of our lives, Satan will seek to find some area of weakness where he can entrench himself and create havoc for us. But 2 Corinthians 10:4-5 tells us that we can use the armor of God to demolish those strongholds in our life.

As we read the Scriptures and equip ourselves with the mind of Christ, with the helmet of salvation, God reveals to us those things in our lives that we have not yet given over to Him. And whether it's greed, pride, anger, addiction—whatever the stronghold— God will show us how, in the wisdom of Christ, to begin pulling it down by renewing our mind according to His Word (Romans 12:2).

What does it mean to "renew your mind"?

Your mind is Satan's target. The Bible could not be more clear: "I am afraid that just as Eve was deceived by the serpent's cunning, your minds may somehow be led astray" (2 Corinthians 11:3, NIV). Satan plays mind games with Christians using his craftiness. So we must renew our minds daily, "bringing every thought into captivity to the obedience of Christ" (2 Corinthians 10:5). That means we must be constantly programming our mind and our spirit with godly things. Don't open yourself up to the things that can corrupt you.

Even though we will never reach perfection on this earth, we can determine, by the grace of God, to rework our mental diet so that the godly things available to us will form the major portion of what we think about and what we meditate on. Listen to godly music that has lyrics that are uplifting and encouraging. Have godly conversations. Read godly literature. Renew your mind.

THE SWORD OF THE SPIRIT

Take . . . the sword of the Spirit,
which is the word of God.
Ephesians 6:17

What protection does the sword of the Spirit provide?

Within God's armory we have one offensive weapon with which we are to do battle against the evil one— "the sword of the Spirit, which is the word of God" (Ephesians 6:17).

When Paul wrote to the Ephesians, he used a specific word for "sword"—the Greek word *machaira*. He wasn't talking about what we would think of as a sword today; he was talking about a dagger, which would have been used in hand-to-hand combat. Therefore, the sword of the Spirit *is not to hit something with*. It is a very precision-oriented instrument.[15] Similarly, the Word of God referred to in this passage does not refer to the whole Bible (the *logos*). It refers to a particular part, or promise, of the Word (a *rhema*) to apply to a particular battle situation. In other words, the Bible is an armory in which the individual swords of the Spirit are kept until you need them for close combat with the enemy. But unlike a material sword that you would use to pierce the body, the spiritual sword pierces the heart. A material sword gets duller as you use it, but a spiritual sword gets sharper every time you use it. And Scripture says that those swords are found within the covers of the Bible.

In Matthew 4, when Jesus was attacked by the Tempter, He confronted Satan with three simple words: "It is written …." And then He quoted passages from Deuteronomy. Isn't it interesting that the Lord Jesus, the Son of God, used the Scripture to defeat Satan?

Years ago, my friend Swen Nater and I got together at a restaurant. We talked about the areas where we thought the enemy would come after us, and we took a concordance and researched the Scriptures. We came up with about forty "swords" for each of us, which we stored in the armories of our minds. I'd suggest you do the same. Think of areas in which you know Satan will tempt you, find some Bible verses relating to those areas, write them out on little cards, and put them where you see them often. Memorize them. Internalize them. Learn them by heart, and be ready to use them when the enemy confronts you.

Satan can't do much with people who keep assaulting him with Scripture.

How do I arm myself with the sword of the Spirit?

The Bible is an armory filled with swords of the Spirit. But most Christians visit the "New Armory" more than the "Old Armory." You might think there aren't many swords back in Leviticus, Numbers, or Deuteronomy that can help in battle. But don't forget, when Jesus was tempted by Satan in the wilderness, all three of His swords were pulled from Deuteronomy (Matthew 4:1-11).

If we don't make a practice of reading and meditating on the entire Bible, we're going to miss a lot of good swords to use against the enemy. When we read and study and meditate on the Word of God, we'll find that we have access to God's armory and our choice of swords whenever we need them. But we have to know the swords.

As believers, we need to memorize the Word of God because most of the temptations we face in life don't come while we have a Bible in our hand! But if we have committed the Bible to memory, we will be able to reach into our memory bank and pull out the sword we need to defeat the enemy.

Hebrews 4:12 presents a most graphic portrayal of the power of the Word of God as a sword. Ancient double-edged swords were valuable because they cut both ways—on the down stroke and the back stroke. And their sharpness of point and blade ensured their deep penetration into an enemy's body, even to the marrow, the deepest part of a human bone. Similarly, the Word of God is effective in all directions. And instead of separating joints and marrow, it goes to the heart of soul and spirit. But like a soldier's sword, the Word of God is only active when it is taken up and used.

How can I effectively wield the sword of the Spirit?

In Matthew 4:1-11, we have an example of how Christ used three swords of the Spirit, three particular verses, to defeat the three temptations Satan presented in the wilderness.

Temptation 1:

The first temptation was to turn stones into bread to satisfy His hunger. Remember, Jesus had been fasting for forty days. But Jesus never acted independently of the Father, nor did He perform a miracle to serve Himself. Instead, He took out a sword of the Spirit, Deuteronomy 8:3, and said: "It is written, 'Man shall not live by bread alone, but by every word that proceeds from the mouth of God'" (Matthew 4:4).

Temptation 2:

Next, Satan tempted Jesus to prove He was the Son of God. Instead, Jesus pulled out another sword, Deuteronomy 6:16, and said: "It is written again, 'You shall not tempt the LORD your God'" (Matthew 4:7).

Temptation 3:

Satan told Jesus he would give Him the kingdoms of the world if He would fall down and worship him. But Jesus pulled out one final sword, Deuteronomy 6:13, and said, "Away with you, Satan! For it is written, 'You shall worship the Lord your God, and Him only you shall serve'" (Matthew 4:10).

Jesus resisted the devil with the Word of God, and the devil left him (Matthew 4:11). And we can use the sword of the Spirit just as Jesus did! All we have to do is reach into our armory and pull out the right sword. It is written!

> Resist the devil and
> he will flee from you.
>
> *James 4:7*

How does the sword of the Spirit transform lives?

Haddon Robinson once wrote that "God speaks through the Bible. . . . Through the preaching of the Scriptures, God encounters men and women to bring them to salvation and to richness and ripeness in Christian character."[16] And whether we're reading our Bible, sitting in church, or listening to Christian radio, the sword of the Spirit can change us in a moment. That's the power of the Word of God! It is living and powerful, sharp enough to divide and discern (Hebrews 4:12).

That's why I get excited every time I preach. When I preach the Word of God, I am throwing swords from the Bible. And I know that God can use those swords, those particular verses or promises from the Bible, to transform lives.

For the word of God *is* living and powerful, and sharper than any two-edged sword, piercing even to the division of soul and spirit, and of joints and marrow, and is a discerner of the thoughts and intents of the heart.

Hebrews 4:12

Am I always equipped with God's armor?

Our armor is only useful if we put it on! If we get defeated in the warfare, if we are wounded in an unprotected place because we are without armor, it's not the fault of our Commander in Chief. God has given us everything we need to battle valiantly and victoriously in one Manual—the Bible. The Bible doesn't say, "Wait for God to put it on you" but "Put it on yourself." It is the Christian's personal responsibility to appropriate the armor of God in his or her own life. This war is not something we fight as a group; we're involved in a personal and private battle with Satan. And if we are not individually and personally implementing the armor of God, we are going to be victims instead of victors.

The armor is sitting there just waiting for us to put it on. And we are to be continually arming ourselves for the warfare. Only then will we be prepared to go out and win the battles that will inevitably come against us.

Why do I need to put on the *whole* armor of God?

All six pieces of spiritual armor are necessary for every believer. No part of our life can be left unprotected or exposed.

A pastor in Haiti created the following parable to illustrate for his people the fatal danger of having any part of our spiritual being exposed to the destructive powers of Satan.

> A certain man wanted to sell his house for $2,000. Another man wanted very badly to buy it, but because he was poor, he couldn't afford the full price. After much bargaining, the owner agreed to sell the house for half the original price with just one stipulation: he would retain ownership of one small nail protruding from just over the door.
>
> After several years, the original owner wanted the house back, but the new owner was unwilling to sell. So first the [original] owner

went out, found the carcass of a dead dog, and hung it from the nail he still owned. Soon the house became unlivable, and the family was forced to sell the house to the owner of the nail.[17]

The Haitian pastor told his congregation, "If we leave the Devil with even one small peg in our life, he will return to hang his rotting garbage on it, making it unfit for Christ's habitation."[18]

That is the kind of ruthless enemy we're up against. Do not give him the tiniest toehold in your life. Do not open the door to your heart even a crack. Do not rationalize or excuse any failure to obey the true Lord of your life. And when failures or missteps occur, as they will, confess them immediately and be cleansed "from all unrighteousness" (1 John 1:9).

The only way to protect oneself from Satan's infiltration is to be on the side of the One who is more powerful than he is: "because He who is in you is greater than he who is in the world" (1 John 4:4).

> But put on the Lord Jesus Christ, and make no provision for the flesh, to *fulfill* its lusts.
> Romans 13:14

How do I "put on" Christ?

As we look at the spiritual armor that is listed for us in the book of Ephesians (Ephesians 6:14-17), it is quite apparent that the armor is nothing less than Jesus Christ Himself. In fact, when Paul wrote to the Romans, he said something very similar to what we find in Ephesians. He said in Romans 13:14, "Put on the Lord Jesus Christ."

In essence, Paul is telling us that we are to wear Christ like we wear a suit of clothes.

Ray Stedman suggests this approach: "When I get up in the morning, I put on my clothes, intending them to be part of me all day, to go where I go and do what I do. They cover me and make me presentable to others. That is the purpose of clothes. In the same way, the apostle is saying to us, 'Put on Jesus Christ when you get up in the morning. Make Him a part of your life that day. Intend that He go with you everywhere you go, and that He acts through you in everything you do. Call upon His resources. Live your life IN CHRIST.'"[19]

The Warfare
of Prayer

. . . praying always with all
prayer and supplication
in the Spirit, being
watchful to this end with
all perseverance and
supplication for all
the saints.

Ephesians 6:18

What is the purpose for prayer in God's armory?

Every soldier needs a good communication device, a radio, or a satellite phone. Paul ends his discussion on the body armor of the Christian by saying, "praying always with all prayer and supplication in the Spirit, being watchful to this end with all perseverance and supplication for all the saints."

Praying always ... all prayer ... all perseverance ... for all the saints. In other words, our radios should always be on. The batteries should always be charged. Our prayer lives should be strong, consistent, and sincere. Many battles can only be won on our knees. Perhaps the battle is for a wayward child or a lost loved one. Perhaps the battle is to regain unity and peace in your church. Perhaps the battle is to overcome a bad habit or an addiction. Perhaps the battle is to break open a resistant mission field. The Bible says that the prayers of a righteous person are powerful and effective (James 5:16, NIV).

God intends us to be "more than conquerors,"

but we can't engage in spiritual warfare without spiritual weapons. We can't be strong in ourselves; we have to be strong in the Lord and in the power of His might. We have to be dressed for battle.

Prayer is the energy that enables the warrior to wear the armor and wield the sword. No matter how talented we might be, if we try to fight the spiritual battle Paul describes in Ephesians 6 in the energy of the flesh, we can never be victorious.

> I asked for strength that I might achieve;
>> He made me weak that I might obey.
> I asked for health that I might do great things;
>> He gave me grace that I might do better things.
> I asked for riches that I might be happy;
>> He gave me poverty that I might be wise.
> I asked for power that I might have the praise of men;
>> He gave me weakness that I might feel a need of God.
> I asked for all things that I might enjoy life;
>> He gave me life that I might enjoy all things.
> I received nothing I had asked for;
>> He gave me all that I had hoped for.[20]

Am I really to pray "always"? Is that possible?

*"Praying **always"** ....* These words remind us of 1 Thessalonians 5:17, which says: "Pray without ceasing." That doesn't mean we should constantly walk around muttering prayers all day. But as soldiers, we must keep our two-way radios constantly on. We must keep the line open so that we can contact Headquarters at a moment's notice. We're to be in continual contact with our Commander in Chief. Prayer isn't just something we do for a few minutes in the morning or evening. It's natural for the prayer warrior to be talking to God all day and all night as the needs or thoughts arise.

A chief implication of this kind of prayer is that it is not based on emotion. We don't pray just when we feel particularly spiritual. Rather, we live in the domain of prayer. It is part of the process of living a "sober . . . vigilant" life (1 Peter 5:8), because our adversary the devil is constantly on the prowl for someone to devour. And because we are constantly in danger, we must be constantly in prayer.

Be in communication with God all the time, in all circumstances, and in all places, as if He is right beside you, because He is!

*Praying always with **all prayer***. According to this verse, we can pray on any occasion, in any location, in any situation, and for any supplication. We can offer all kinds of prayers—praises, petitions, confessions, prayers of anguish and prayers of exaltation, long prayers and short prayers, individual prayers and group prayers. We can pray aloud and silently. We can write our prayers and sing our prayers. We can make prayer an exciting adventure rather than a boring routine.

*Praying always with all prayer **and supplication***. This word "supplication" means asking God for what you need. James warned that we have not because we ask not. That's why we keep prayer lists, and that's why we share our prayer requests with others. Asking is the rule of the kingdom, for God has the resources to meet our needs.

In the little anonymous book, *The Kneeling Christian*,

we read: "Prayer is the key that unlocks the door of God's treasure-house. It is not too much to say that all real growth in the spiritual life—all victory over temptation, all confidence and peace in the presence of difficulties and dangers, all repose of spirit during times of great disappointment or loss, all habitual communion with God—depends on the practice of secret prayer."

One of the first books that I chose to read on prayer was a book by Bill Hybels entitled *Too Busy Not to Pray*. I wanted to read this book because the title intrigued me; it sounded like an anomaly, a contradiction in terms. At the beginning of chapter one, Hybels writes:

> Prayer is an unnatural activity. From birth we have been learning the rules of self-reliance as we strain and struggle to achieve self-sufficiency. Prayer flies in the face of those deep-seated values. It is an assault on human autonomy, an indictment of independent living. To people in the fast lane, determined to make it on their own, prayer is an embarrassing interruption.[21]

What does it mean to be "watchful" in prayer?

Paul's words in Ephesians 6:18 suggest that prayer requires care and diligence, that it is an extremely important dimension of the Christian life. Anything we "watch over" is something of great importance to us. And prayer definitely falls into that category.

A prayerful life does not consist of just the words we say to God. It begins long before we start to pray—it begins with the attitude of our heart, our relationships with others, the thoughts we meditate on during the day. Prayer is a reflection of our entire life. We must permit nothing into our life that would make us unfit for coming before God's "throne of grace" (Hebrews 4:16). The life of prayer is a watchful life in which we take care not to do anything that would hinder our communication with God.

The Greek word for "watchful" has at its root meaning the absence of sleep due to remaining watchful for something—watching for an animal when hunting or watching for an enemy. It signifies an alert, wakeful frame of mind, the state required for someone who is guarding something as opposed to a casual, relaxed attitude. It is entirely consistent with the perspective needed by one engaged in spiritual warfare.

It's easy to find our mind wandering or our mind getting drowsy when we pray. I have found that I can pray much more alertly and carefully when I am outdoors, perhaps taking a walk, than on my knees. I pray on my knees as well, of course; but depending on the time of day, I can fight off "sleep" better by "prayer walking." Whatever we have to do to remain alert and watchful when we pray—we should do it. God wants the attention of our hearts and minds so that He can fill us with His strength as we engage in spiritual warfare.

The warrior must be vigilant in his prayer life. We must permit nothing to disrupt it. The warrior guards his time, plans his schedule, watches for everything that feeds the prayer life, and guards against anything that will distract from praying. I've found that reading a chapter from a book about prayer each day helps prepare my heart for praying. It's like priming the pump.

Prayer itself is a part of
spiritual warfare—it is the
lifeblood for those who
seek to be victorious.

How does Satan attempt to attack my prayer life?

Prayer itself is a part of spiritual warfare—it is the lifeblood for those who seek to be victorious. And Satan would like nothing better than to keep us from praying through distractions, discouragement, delays, or disappointment. Satan is a master at deception and discouragement. For instance, if you have two productive days of watchful prayer, Satan might try to convince you that you have finally mastered the discipline of prayer. Then, on the third day when you fail at being watchful in prayer, he will tell you that you're a failure—you've blown it and there is no use trying any further. If you miss one day in fruitful prayer, Satan can try to convince you that you are beyond help and hope—that you needn't try again. But the good news is, there's a secret to overcoming Satan's deception. As with any other area of the spiritual life, if you fail, the thing to do is to begin again. There is no permanent failure in learning to be a faithful disciple of Jesus. If you have a bad day in your prayer life, purpose to begin again! Don't give in to the devil's tactics that are designed to keep you from praying.

The enemy of our souls wants to keep us from developing a relationship that he knows will bring joy and satisfaction to us. But by the grace of God, we need to determine that we are going to keep on praying. Only in the process of praying will we find the meaning of life: a dynamic, personal relationship with the Creator, the living Lord, the Babe of Bethlehem, the Savior of the Cross, the resurrection morning Victor, the only One who is life to us.

Billy Graham tells of a woman who wrote that she had pleaded in prayer for ten years for the conversion of her husband, but that he was more hardened than ever. Mr. Graham advised her to keep praying. One day he received another letter. The husband had been gloriously saved. "Suppose she had stopped after only ten years," said the evangelist. Then he added, "Never stop praying no matter how dark and hopeless your case may seem."

What does it mean to be a "prayer warrior"?

Prayer is work—and it requires all-out battle. It is not an idle pastime or an optional exercise reserved for more "spiritual" believers. Prayer is the hard-work business of the Church of Jesus Christ. The kind of prayer that changes hearts and transforms neighborhoods and rebuilds communities and revives nations is intense, fervent, and all business. It takes a proactive commitment on our part to set aside the time and effort to be strong in prayer and to give energy to our praying. Colossians 4:2 says we are to "continue earnestly in prayer." That's what it means to be a "prayer warrior." Hand-to-hand combat with issues of daily living, fiercely fought in front of our Father—that is what committed Christian prayer looks like.

I've learned that Satan trembles when he sees the least of God's children on their knees. Praise given to God causes the enemy to be incredibly uncomfortable. Whatever he wants to do, he has to work ten times harder to do it when God's people are praying.

How can I know what to pray for?

The whole idea behind prayer is that we pray according to God's will. So how can we know what to pray? The answer is: the indwelling Holy Spirit. The same Holy Spirit who inspired the writing of the Word of God lives in every born-again follower of Christ. It is He who helps shape our prayers—as we submit them to Him—to be in accordance with the will and Word of God (Romans 8:26-27). As we saturate our mind and heart with the Word of God, we grow in our sense of what the will of God is— what God would do if He were in our place. Just as a child learns what things to ask or not to ask of his father, so we learn how to ask according to our Father's will. And the Spirit comes alongside to help us pray when we are unsure or cannot find the words.

Recently I read these words about prayer written by Alan Redpath, "Before we can pray, 'Thy Kingdom come,' we must be willing to pray—'my kingdom go!'"

He who searches the
hearts knows what
the mind of the Spirit
is, because He makes
intercession for the
saints according to
the will of God.

Romans 8:27

Is there a model for prayer?

God longs for His people to communicate with Him, to talk to Him in the same way we would speak with the most precious person in our life. He doesn't want vain repetitions; He wants real communication (Matthew 6:7). Jesus teaches us to approach God honestly, openly, and sincerely. There are no "special words" we must use before we're allowed into God's presence. Yet, if we are to pray effectively, there are some key ideas to keep in mind; and that's what the Lord's Prayer is all about.

The Lord's Prayer (Matthew 6:9-13) is a model for us to follow in our prayer lives. If we get this remarkable prayer down deep into our hearts and minds where it belongs, it will change our lives. It wasn't created to make us feel guilty or unworthy but to show us the proper and most effective way to enter the very throne room of God Almighty. Incredible as it may seem, God is waiting to hear from us. He wants us to come boldly into His presence. And this prayer shows us the way.

～

Our Father in heaven, hallowed
be Your name. Your kingdom
come. Your will be done on
earth as *it is* in heaven. Give us
this day our daily bread. And
forgive us our debts, as we
forgive our debtors. And do not
lead us into temptation, but
deliver us from the evil one. For
Yours is the kingdom and the
power and the glory forever.
Amen.

Matthew 6:9-13

～

How can I develop an effective prayer life?

It's one thing to be told to do something; it's even more helpful to be shown how to do it. But the best way to learn anything is by practicing it ourselves. The best way to learn to pray as Jesus taught is to start praying today—using the pattern of the Lord's Prayer.

The Lord's Prayer is the most famous prayer in the world. It should more accurately be called the Disciples' Prayer since the prayer asks for forgiveness of sins—and we know Christ never sinned. It is the Lord's Prayer because He taught it, not because He prayed it.

There are just 66 words in this prayer, but it has become the basis of countless sermons, books, and even songs. Andrew Murray once said, "It is a form of prayer that becomes the model and the inspiration for all other prayers, and yet always draws us back to itself as the deepest utterance of our souls before God." The Lord's Prayer is perfectly balanced. It teaches us to look first to God, then to ourselves. It teaches us to forgive and receive forgiveness. And it teaches us to depend wholly upon God for everything.

The Lord did not give us this prayer so that we would memorize it and repeat it mindlessly as a ritual. He gave it to us as an outline to follow when we pray. Several years ago I organized this prayer to use in my own prayer life and I include this outline to encourage you to pray as our Lord has taught us to pray.

Practical Application of the Disciples' Prayer

(Matthew 6:5-15)

PERSPECTIVE

Before I start the journey, I have decided . . .

- Not to Pray Like the Hypocrites—"They love to pray . . . that they may be seen . . ." Matthew 6:5

- Not to Pray Like the Heathen—"They think they will be heard for their many words." Matthew 6:7

PRAISE

Our Father which art in heaven, Hallowed be thy name
"Enter into His gates with thanksgiving, and into His courts with praise." Psalm 100:4

I Will Hallow His Name By . . .

- **Rehearsing His Names:**

  Jehovah Tsidkenu, Jehovah Our Righteousness
  (Jeremiah 23:6)

  Jehovah Mekaddishkhem, Jehovah Who Sanctifies
  (Leviticus 20:7-8)

  Jehovah Shalom, Jehovah Who Is Our Peace
  (Judges 6:24)

  Jehovah Shammah, Jehovah Is There, He Never
  Leaves Us (Ezekiel 48:35)

  Jehovah Rophe, The Lord Who Heals
  (Exodus 15:26)

  Jehovah-Jireh, The Lord Who Provides
  (Genesis 22:14)

  Jehovah-Nissi, The Lord my Banner
  (Exodus 17:15)

  Jehovah Roi, The Lord Who Is My Shepherd
  (Psalm 23:1)

- **Respecting His Greatness: His Attributes**

  Eternal - Psalm 90:2
  Righteous - Psalm 11:7
  Good - Matthew 19:17
  Unchanging - Malachi 3:6
  Sovereign - Ephesians 1:11
  Faithful - Lamentations 3:23
  All-powerful - Revelation 19:6
  Ever-present - Psalm 139:7-11
  Longsuffering - Psalm 86:15
  Holy - Psalm 99:3
  True - John 17:3
  Love - I John 4:8
  All-knowing - Acts 15:18
  Kind - Psalm 31:21

- **Recognizing His Presence:**

  "I have set the Lord always before me. . . ."
  Psalm 16:8

P RIORITIES

Thy kingdom come. Thy will be done in earth, as it is in heaven.
"But seek first the kingdom of God and His righteousness, and all these things shall be added to you." Matthew 6:33

- **I Will Remember That . . .**

  1. I am a Person—I have a relationship with God.

  2. I am a Partner—I have a relationship with my spouse.

  3. I am a Parent—I have a relationship with my children.

  4. I am a Provider—I have a responsibility in my job/ profession.

  5. I am a Participant—I have a responsibility in other things I am asked to do.

PROVISION

Give us this day our daily bread.
"Ask, and it will be given to you; Seek, and you will find; Knock, and it will be opened to you." Luke 11:9

- I Will Depend on God for My Needs—Psalm 104:27, James 1:17

- I Will Distinguish Between Needs and Wants.
  ". . . our daily bread. . . ." (I Timothy 6:8)
  Something to put on—clothes
  Something to put in—food
  Something to put over—shelter

- I Will Discipline Myself Not to Worry.
  "Give us . . . our daily bread." Day to day, not

week to week, or month to month, or year
to year.

- I Will Defer to the Needs of Others.
  "Give us . . . ," not me. "Give us our . . . ,"
  not my.

PERSONAL RELATIONSHIPS

And forgive us our debts, as we forgive our debtors.
"For if you forgive men their trespasses, your
heavenly Father will also forgive you. But if you do
not forgive men their trespasses, neither will your
Father forgive your trespasses." Matthew 6:14-15

- We Are to Forgive Because We Are Forgiven.
  Matthew 18:21-35 explains the importance of
  forgiving one another.

- We Are to Forgive Just As We Are Forgiven.
  Ephesians 4:32

- We Are to Forgive in Order that We Might Be
  Forgiven. (Psalm 66:18)

- We Are to Forgive Before We Need to Be
  Forgiven—At the start of each day we
  remember our forgiveness and determine
  to forgive those who will hurt us.

- We Are to Forgive Always, and It Is Always
  Our Turn.
  How often? (Matthew 18:22).
  Who initiates? (Matthew 18:25, Mark 11:25)

P ROTECTION

*And lead us not into temptation, but deliver us
from evil.*

Six Steps of Temptation
1. Deceit
2. Delight
3. Desire
4. Deliberation
5. Defeat
6. Despair

Overcoming Temptation
1. Fight—James 4:7
2. Follow—James 4:8
3. Flee—2 Timothy 2:22, Romans 13:14
4. Feed—Psalm 119:11

Deliverance from Evil

- Deliverance from persecution—Psalm 22:19
- Deliverance from peril—Psalm 31:1-2, 15
- Deliverance from problems—Psalm 34:4, 17
  "The Lord knows how to deliver the godly out of temptations." 2 Peter 2:9

PRAISE AGAIN

For thine is the kingdom, and the power, and the glory, forever. Amen.

- Lord, I praise You for Your sovereignty.
  thine is the kingdom . . .

- Lord, I praise You for Your authority.
  . . . and the power . . .

- Lord, I praise You for Your majesty.
  . . . and the glory . . .

- Lord, I praise You for Your eternality.
  . . . forever . . .

— Amen —

Why should I continue to pray when I feel God isn't answering my prayers?

We err when we judge our prayers solely by what we can see happening around us. Prayer is a matter of faith. Prayer is taking God at His word and understanding God's promise that if we pray, He will work. And we must keep on praying even when we cannot see what He is doing. We do not see into the world in which God lives, but He definitely sees into ours. By our praying, we are giving evidence that we have committed ourselves to Him, that we take God at His word, that we trust Him, and that even though we can't always see what He is doing, we know He is working in our life.

> He shall call upon Me, and I will answer him; I will be with him in trouble; I will deliver him and honor him. With long life I will satisfy him, and show him My salvation.
> *Psalm 91:15-16*

What are some ways I can pray for others?

In Ephesians 6, Paul's admonition about the importance of prayer is to pray "for all the saints." Every Christian is included in "all the saints." And if we compare how Paul prayed for people with how we often pray for others, we might be surprised. Oftentimes we pray for people to be healed of their sickness, find a good job, have a safe vacation, restore a relationship, and so on—things that have to do with our personal comfort level as individuals. Our prayers tend to be focused on the material, physical aspects of life. That's not to say God isn't concerned about those parts of our life, but He is also concerned about the deeper, more spiritual parts. The apostle Paul prayed continually for the saints in the churches he founded and ministered to; and when he prayed, he focused on the spiritual, non-material aspects of life. He prayed for increased love, power, discernment, and knowledge of God's will—the very things Satan would attempt to take away from Christians in order to confuse, weaken, or discourage them (Ephesians 1:18-19; 3:16-19; Philippians 1:9-11; Colossians 1:9; 1 Thessalonians 3:10-13; 2 Thessalonians 2:16-17).

As we pray for "all the saints," let's remember these deeper spiritual realities. That is where spiritual warfare is going to be either won or lost.

> Strategic warfare prayer
> needs a place, a purpose,
> a plan—but most of all,
> someone to pray.

How can I persevere in the battle when I'm afraid?

I know what it's like to have a "fear day." Sometimes, suddenly and out of nowhere, the spirit of fear grips my heart and I have to drop everything and tell God about my fear, asking Him to deliver me from it. Fear is paralyzing. Fear can keep us from doing the things God wants us to do. That's why Jesus tells us to pray for deliverance from evil. When fear strikes, give it to God with a simple prayer: "Lord, deliver me from evil, including all my fear. This situation is beyond me. I can't cope with it. But You can. Please extend Your hand, and by Your power, help me and deliver me."

Whenever I am afraid, I will trust in You.
Psalm 56:3

Behold, God is my salvation, I will trust and not be afraid; for YAH, the LORD, is my strength and song; He also has become my salvation.
Isaiah 12:2

Conclusion

How should I live today in light of the battle before me?

Day by day the battle is heating up and the challenges are becoming greater; but we're not in doubt as to how it's going to turn out. God has given us a hope that is secure, steadfast, and that can never be touched. It is beyond decay or destruction. Because Jesus Christ is eternal, our hope in Him is eternal. And we can live in hope if we understand and believe the truth concerning the risen Christ. We have a living hope, a hope based upon what Jesus Christ did when He arose from the grave. He gained victory over death.

By virtue of that accomplishment, Jesus has laid claim to our faith and says in effect, "If I came out of the grave victorious over death, and you put your trust in Me, you can have that same victory—not only over death, but in your life, day by day." We are victors through Christ! We just need to start acting like it. We are God's people, and Satan does not have any claim to us unless we give it to him. And the way we keep that from happening is by putting on the whole armor of God every day so that we might be able to stand against the evil one, "and having done all, to stand."

> Therefore take up the whole armor of God, that you may be able to withstand in the evil day, and having done all, to stand.
>
> *Ephesians 6:13*

The Warrior's Prayer

The precision of "The Warrior's Prayer" will help you put on each piece of spiritual armor with purpose and start each day in communion with God. When we remain persistent and focused in prayer, our eyes begin to open to the power of Christ in our lives, and we become armed for victory!

Heavenly Father,

Your warrior prepares for battle.

Today I claim victory

over Satan by putting on

the whole armor of God!

I put on the Girdle of Truth!

May I stand firm in

the truth of Your Word

so I will not be a victim

of Satan's lies.

I put on the Breastplate of Righteousness!

May it guard my heart from evil

so I will remain pure and holy,

protected under the blood

of Jesus Christ.

I put on the Shoes of Peace!

May I stand firm in

the good news of the Gospel

so Your peace will shine

through me and be a light

to all I encounter.

I take the Shield of Faith!

May I be ready for Satan's fiery darts

of doubt, denial, and deceit

so I will not be vulnerable

to spiritual defeat.

*I put on the Helmet
of Salvation!*

May I keep my mind focused

on You so Satan will not

have a stronghold on

my thoughts.

I take the Sword of the Spirit!

May the two-edged sword
of Your Word be ready in my hands
so I can expose the tempting
words of Satan.

*By faith Your warrior
has put on the whole
armor of God!*

I am prepared to live this day

in spiritual victory!

Amen.

Scripture
Reference
Guide

Spiritual Warfare
Scripture Reference Guide

Deuteronomy 20:1 When you go out to battle against your enemies, and see horses and chariots *and* people more numerous than you, do not be afraid of them; for the LORD your God *is* with you, who brought you up from the land of Egypt.

2 Samuel 22:3-4 The God of my strength, in whom I will trust; my shield and the horn of my salvation, my stronghold and my refuge; my Savior, You save me from violence. I will call upon the LORD, *who is worthy* to be praised; so shall I be saved from my enemies.

Psalm 27:3 Though an army may encamp against me, my heart shall not fear; though war may rise against me, in this I *will be* confident.

Psalm 44:5 Through You we will push down our enemies; through Your name we will trample those who rise up against us.

Psalm 46:1-2 God *is* our refuge and strength, a very present help in trouble. Therefore we will not fear, even though the earth be removed, and though the mountains be carried into the midst of the sea.

Psalm 60:11-12 Give us help from trouble, for the help of man *is* useless. Through God we will do valiantly, for *it is* He *who* shall tread down our enemies.

Psalm 121:7-8 The LORD shall preserve you from all evil; He shall preserve your soul. The LORD shall preserve your going out and your coming in from this time forth, and even forevermore.

Proverbs 25:28 Whoever *has* no rule over his own spirit *is like* a city broken down, without walls.

Isaiah 41:10 Fear not, for I *am* with you; be not dismayed, for I *am* your God. I will strengthen you, yes, I will help you, I will uphold you with My righteous right hand.

Isaiah 54:17 "No weapon formed against you shall prosper, and every tongue *which* rises against you in judgment you shall condemn. This *is* the heritage of the servants of the LORD, and their righteousness *is* from Me," says the LORD.

Matthew 6:13 And do not lead us into temptation, but deliver us from the evil one. For Yours is the kingdom and the power and the glory forever. Amen.

Matthew 18:18 Assuredly, I say to you, whatever you bind on earth will be bound in heaven, and whatever you loose on earth will be loosed in heaven.

Luke 10:19 Behold, I give you the authority to trample on serpents and scorpions, and over all the power of the enemy, and nothing shall by any means hurt you.

John 10:10 The thief does not come except to steal, and to kill, and to destroy. I have come that they may have life, and that they may have *it* more abundantly.

John 16:33 These things I have spoken to you, that in Me you may have peace. In the world you will have tribulation; but be of good cheer, I have overcome the world.

Romans 8:5-6 For those who live according to the flesh set their minds on the things of the flesh, but those *who live* according to the Spirit, the things of the Spirit. For to be carnally minded *is* death, but to be spiritually minded *is* life and peace.

Romans 8:31 What then shall we say to these things? If God *is* for us, who *can be* against us?

Romans 8:35 Who shall separate us from the love of Christ? *Shall* tribulation, or distress, or persecution, or famine, or nakedness, or peril, or sword?

Romans 8:38-39 For I am persuaded that neither death nor life, nor angels nor principalities nor powers, nor things present nor things to come, nor height nor depth, nor any other created thing, shall be able to separate us from the love of God which is in Christ Jesus our Lord.

Romans 12:2 And do not be conformed to this world, but be transformed by the renewing of your mind, that you may prove what *is* that good and acceptable and perfect will of God.

Romans 12:21 Do not be overcome by evil, but overcome evil with good.

1 Corinthians 15:57 But thanks *be* to God, who gives us the victory through our Lord Jesus Christ.

1 Corinthians 16:13 Watch, stand fast in the faith, be brave, be strong.

2 Corinthians 1:3-4 Blessed *be* the God and Father of our Lord Jesus Christ, the Father of mercies and God of all comfort, who comforts us in all our tribulation, that we may be able to comfort those who are in any trouble, with the comfort with which we ourselves are comforted by God.

2 Corinthians 4:3-4 But even if our gospel is veiled, it is veiled to those who are perishing, whose minds the god of this age has blinded, who do not believe, lest the light of the gospel of the glory of Christ, who is the image of God, should shine on them.

2 Corinthians 7:1 Therefore, having these promises, beloved, let us cleanse ourselves from all filthiness of the flesh and spirit, perfecting holiness in the fear of God.

2 Corinthians 10:3-5 For though we walk in the flesh, we do not war according to the flesh. For the weapons of our warfare *are* not carnal but mighty in God for pulling down strongholds, casting down arguments and every high thing that exalts itself against the knowledge of God, bringing every thought into captivity to the obedience of Christ.

Galatians 5:17 For the flesh lusts against the Spirit, and the Spirit against the flesh; and these are contrary to one another, so that you do not do the things that you wish.

Galatians 5:24-25 And those *who are* Christ's have crucified the flesh with its passions and desires. If we live in the Spirit, let us also walk in the Spirit.

Ephesians 4:26-27 "Be angry, and do not sin": do not let the sun go down on your wrath, nor give place to the devil.

Ephesians 6:10-11 Finally, my brethren, be strong in the Lord and in the power of His might. Put on the whole armor of God, that you may be able to stand against the wiles of the devil.

Ephesians 6:12-13 For we do not wrestle against flesh and blood, but against principalities, against powers, against the rulers of the darkness of this age, against spiritual *hosts* of wickedness in the heavenly *places*. Therefore take up the whole armor of God, that you may be able to withstand in the evil day, and having done all, to stand.

Ephesians 6:14-17 Stand therefore, having girded your waist with truth, having put on the breastplate of righteousness, and having shod your feet with the preparation of the gospel of peace; above all, taking the shield of faith with which you will be able to quench all the fiery darts of the wicked one. And take the helmet of salvation, and the sword of the Spirit, which is the word of God.

Colossians 1:13 He has delivered us from the power of darkness and conveyed *us* into the kingdom of the Son of His love.

Colossians 2:15 Having disarmed principalities and powers, He made a public spectacle of them, triumphing over them in it.

2 Thessalonians 3:3 But the Lord is faithful, who will establish you and guard *you* from the evil one.

1 Timothy 6:12 Fight the good fight of faith, lay hold on eternal life, to which you were also called and have confessed the good confession in the presence of many witnesses.

2 Timothy 1:7 For God has not given us a spirit of fear, but of power and of love and of a sound mind.

2 Timothy 4:18 And the Lord will deliver me from every evil work and preserve *me* for His heavenly kingdom. To Him *be* glory forever and ever. Amen!

James 1:2-4 My brethren, count it all joy when you fall into various trials, knowing that the testing of your faith produces patience. But let patience have *its* perfect work, that you may be perfect and complete, lacking nothing.

James 4:7-8 Therefore submit to God. Resist the devil and he will flee from you. Draw near to God and He will draw near to you. Cleanse *your* hands, *you* sinners; and purify *your* hearts, *you* double-minded.

1 Peter 4:16 Yet if *anyone suffers* as a Christian, let him not be ashamed, but let him glorify God in this matter.

1 Peter 5:8-9 Be sober, be vigilant; because your adversary the devil walks about like a roaring lion, seeking whom he may devour. Resist him, steadfast in the faith, knowing that the same sufferings are experienced by your brotherhood in the world.

1 John 4:4 You are of God, little children, and have overcome them, because He who is in you is greater than he who is in the world.

1 John 5:19 We know that we are of God, and the whole world lies *under the sway of* the wicked one.

Prayer Scripture Reference Guide

2 Chronicles 7:14 If My people who are called by My name will humble themselves, and pray and seek My face, and turn from their wicked ways, then I will hear from heaven, and will forgive their sin and heal their land.

Psalm 4:1 Hear me when I call, O God of my righteousness! You have relieved me in *my* distress; have mercy on me, and hear my prayer.

Psalm 6:8-10 Depart from me, all you workers of iniquity; for the LORD has heard the voice of my weeping. The LORD has heard my supplication; the LORD will receive my prayer. Let all my enemies be ashamed and greatly troubled; let them turn back *and* be ashamed suddenly.

Psalm 18:3 I will call upon the LORD, *who is worthy* to be praised; so shall I be saved from my enemies.

Psalm 55:16 As for me, I will call upon God, and the LORD shall save me.

Psalm 61:1-2 Hear my cry, O God; attend to my prayer. From the end of the earth I will cry to You, when my heart is overwhelmed; lead me to the rock that is higher than I.

Psalm 118:5 I called on the LORD in distress; the LORD answered me *and set me* in a broad place.

Psalm 145:18 The LORD *is* near to all who call upon Him, to all who call upon Him in truth.

Proverbs 15:29 The LORD *is* far from the wicked, but He hears the prayer of the righteous.

Matthew 5:44 But I say to you, love your enemies, bless those who curse you, do good to those who hate you, and pray for those who spitefully use you and persecute you.

Matthew 26:41 Watch and pray, lest you enter into temptation. The spirit indeed *is* willing, but the flesh *is* weak.

Mark 11:24 Therefore I say to you, whatever things you ask when you pray, believe that you receive *them*, and you will have *them*.

Mark 14:38 Watch and pray, lest you enter into temptation. The spirit indeed *is* willing, but the flesh *is* weak.

Luke 21:36 Watch therefore, and pray always that you may be counted worthy to escape all these things that will come to pass, and to stand before the Son of Man.

Romans 12:12 Rejoicing in hope, patient in tribulation, continuing steadfastly in prayer.

Ephesians 6:18 Praying always with all prayer and supplication in the Spirit, being watchful to this end with all perseverance and supplication for all the saints.

Philippians 4:6-7 Be anxious for nothing, but in everything by prayer and supplication, with thanksgiving, let your requests be made known to God; and the peace of God, which surpasses all understanding, will guard your hearts and minds through Christ Jesus.

Colossians 1:9 For this reason we also, since the day we heard it, do not cease to pray for you, and to ask that you may be filled with the knowledge of His will in all wisdom and spiritual understanding.

Colossians 4:2 Continue earnestly in prayer, being vigilant in it with thanksgiving.

1 Thessalonians 5:16-18 Rejoice always, pray without ceasing, in everything give thanks; for this is the will of God in Christ Jesus for you.

2 Thessalonians 3:1-2 Finally, brethren, pray for us, that the word of the Lord may run *swiftly* and be glorified, just as *it is* with you, and that we may be delivered from unreasonable and wicked men; for not all have faith.

Hebrews 5:7 In the days of His flesh, when He had offered up prayers and supplications, with vehement cries and tears to Him who was able to save Him from death, and was heard because of His godly fear.

James 5:13 Is anyone among you suffering? Let him pray. Is anyone cheerful? Let him sing psalms.

1 John 5:14 Now this is the confidence that we have in Him, that if we ask anything according to His will, He hears us.

Jude 1:20 But you, beloved, building yourselves up on your most holy faith, praying in the Holy Spirit.

Additional Resources From Dr. Jeremiah

What Are You Afraid Of?

Fear often arises involuntarily in the face of unwanted circumstances. For many people, worry and anxiety keep them from the life God has called them to. But fear can be overcome through faith in our heavenly Father. In *What Are You Afraid Of*, Dr. Jeremiah discusses nine fears we should *overcome* along with one fear we should *embrace*—the fear of God.

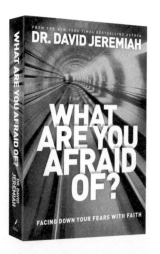

Slaying the Giants in Your Life

Giants—fear, loneliness, worry, doubt—plague many lives in our world today. These giants cause many Christians to stumble, falling away from God's path. In *Slaying the Giants in Your Life*, Dr. Jeremiah uses real-life stories to show you God's promise of protection so that you can slay the giants in your life.

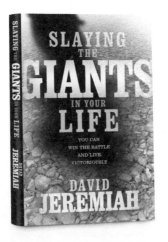

Two great ways to order:

 800-947-1993   DavidJeremiah.org

Living With Confidence in a Chaotic World

Our world is filled with chaos. Natural disasters and moral depravity are on the rise, and violence happens all around us. So what do we do now? In *Living With Confidence in a Chaotic World*, Dr. Jeremiah brings us hope through God's Word by helping us stay centered on Christ. His love and power are all we need to live with confidence in this world.

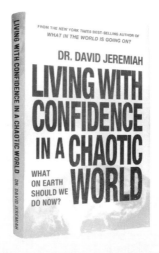

Overcoming Loneliness

Nobody is exempt from the pain loneliness brings. Some even feel its physical effects in the pit of their stomach. Whatever the effect, we are all susceptible to loneliness. In this book, Dr. Jeremiah suggests ways to help you heal and provides reassurance that God is there, helping you overcome your loneliness.

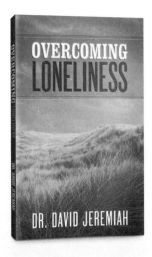

Two great ways to order:

 800-947-1993   DavidJeremiah.org

About Dr. David Jeremiah

Dr. David Jeremiah serves as senior pastor of
Shadow Mountain Community Church in El Cajon,
California. He is the founder and host of *Turning
Point*, a ministry committed to providing Christians
with sound Bible teaching relevant to today's
changing times through radio and television, the
Internet, live events, and resource materials and
books. A best-selling author, Dr. Jeremiah has
written more than forty books including *Captured*

by Grace, *Living with Confidence in a Chaotic World*, *What in the World Is Going On?*, *The Coming Economic Armageddon*, *God Loves You—He Always Has. He Always Will*, and *What Are You Afraid Of?*

Dr. Jeremiah's commitment to teaching the complete Word of God continues to make him a sought-after speaker and writer. His passion for reaching the lost and encouraging believers in their faith is demonstrated through his faithful communication of biblical truths.

A dedicated family man, Dr. Jeremiah and his wife, Donna, have four grown children and eleven grandchildren.

Topical Index

Endnotes

1. J. C. Ryle, *Holiness* (Chicago: Moody, 2010), 115.

2. Stu Weber, *Spirit Warriors* (Sisters, OR: Multnomah Publishers, 2001), 10.

3. Albert J. Hough, "Don't Believe in a Devil" (1889, Public Domain).

4. John Phillips, *Exploring Ephesians and Philippians: An Expository Commentary* (Grand Rapids, MI: Kregel Publications, 1995), 187.

5. J. C. Ryle, *Holiness*, 115.

6. J. C. Ryle, *Holiness*, 118.

7. Sun Tzu, *The Art of War* (Hollywood, FL: Simon and Brown, 2010), 11.

8. Terry Law, *The Truth About Angels* (Lake Mary, FL: Charisma House, 1994, 2006), 126.

9. C. S. Lewis, *Mere Christianity* (San Francisco: HarperCollins, 1952), 121.

10. D. M. Lloyd-Jones, *The Christian Warfare* (Grand Rapids: Baker Book House, 1977), 20-21.

11. R. Kent Hughes, *Ephesians: The Mystery of the Body of Christ* (Wheaton, IL: Crossway, 1990), 217.

12. Roger Olson, The Story of Christian Theology (InterVarsity Press, 1999), 20-21.

13. Weber, *Spirit Warriors*, 172.

14. Tremper Longman, *How to Read Proverbs* (Downers Grove, IL: InterVarsity Press, 2002), 14.

15. John MacArthur, *How to Meet the Enemy: Arming Yourself for Spiritual Warfare* (Colorado Springs: Victor Books, 1992), 141.

16. Haddon Robinson, *Biblical Preaching* (Grand Rapids: Baker Books, 2001), 20.

17. Craig Brian Larson, *Leadership Journal, 750 Engaging Illustration for Preachers, Teachers, and Writers* (Grand Rapids: Baker Books, 2002), 70.

18. Ibid.

19. Ray Stedman, *From Guilt to Glory*, Volume 21 (Waco, TX: Word, 1978), 136.

20. Michael P. Green, ed., *Illustrations for Biblical Preaching*, "Prayer, Answers to" (Grand Rapids: Baker Book House, 1991), 274.

21. Bill Hybels, *Too Busy Not to Pray* (Downers Grove, IL: InterVarsity Press, 1998), 9.

- Notes -